To the Teacher

W9-AXM-593

The *Taking Off* Literacy Workbook has been designed for literacy students enrolled in low beginning classes. Most low beginning students are true beginners in English who are literate in their first language. Literacy students, on the other hand, usually do not have fundamental first-language literacy skills. Literacy students often need specific instruction in letter formation, phonics, and other fundamental reading, listening, and writing skills.

As teachers who have worked with mixed groups of literacy and low beginning students know, dealing simultaneously with the needs of each of these groups of learners is a great challenge. The Literacy Workbook offers a unique resource for teachers in such multi-level classes. Working with or without a teacher's aide, literacy students can tackle basic reading, listening, and writing activities in the Literacy Workbook while students who already have literacy skills can take on the tasks in the Workbook.

The *Taking Off* Literacy Workbook is divided into three sections. Section 1 contains 37 pages of basic literacy and numeracy exercises. These exercises focus on visual and aural identification of the alphabet, writing uppercase and lowercase letters, and the numerals 0 to 10. Section 2, *Phonics Practice,* is completely new to this edition. It contains 26 pages of basic letter-sound associations for consonants and short vowels. The new *Phonics Practice* section is supported by extensive art. It also includes a long-vowel reference chart. Section 3 contains six pages of literacy support for key elements in each of the corresponding units of the Student Book, including support for new *Grammar, Read,* and *Write* pages.

Special audiocassettes and CDs for the Literacy Workbook offer additional listening practice for literacy students.

Table of Contents

Taking Off
Literacy Workbook
Second Edition

Susan Hancock Fesler   Christy M. Newman

Taking Off Literacy Workbook, 2nd Edition

Published by McGraw-Hill ESL/ELT, a business unit of The McGraw-Hill Companies, Inc., 1221 Avenue of the Americas, New York, NY 10020. Copyright © 2008 by The McGraw-Hill Companies, Inc. All rights reserved. No part of this publication may be reproduced or distributed in any form or by any means, or stored in a database or retrieval system, without the prior written consent of The McGraw-Hill Companies, Inc., including, but not limited to, in any network or other electronic storage or transmission, or broadcast for distance learning.

This book is printed on recycled, acid-free paper containing 10% postconsumer waste.

ISBN 13: 978-0-07-331433-4
ISBN 10: 0-07-331433-1
8 9 10 WDQ 11 10

Project manager: Linda O'Roke
Developmental editor: Jennifer Wilson Cooper
Cover designer: Wee Design
Interior designer: Aptara
Artists: Anna Divito, Roberta Rieple, Nancy Carpenter, Fred Bell

Copyright © 2008. Exclusive rights by The McGraw-Hill Companies, Inc. for manufacture and export. This book cannot be re-exported from the country to which it was sold by McGraw-Hill. The International Edition is not available in North America.

www.esl_elt.mcgraw-hill.com

Cover image: Anna Divito

Table of Contents

Table of Contents

Table of Contents

Table of Contents

A Listen.

T   I   L   H

Listen and repeat.

B Circle.

1. T   (T)   H   I   (T)   L   (T)   H
2. I   I   T   L   H   I   T   I
3. L   L   I   L   H   G   I   L
4. H   I   H   L   T   H   H   I

C Copy.

T

I

L

H

A Listen.

E F A Y X

Listen and repeat.

B Circle.

1. E (E) H F (E) T L (E)
2. F I F E H F F E
3. A Y A Y A X A H
4. Y Y X A H Y Z Y
5. X A X H X Y X H

C Copy.

E E E

F F F

A A A

Y Y Y

X X X

N M V W K

 **A** **Listen.**

N   M   V   W   K

Listen and repeat.

B **Circle.**

1. N (N) M X (N) (N) W Y
2. M W M V M X M A
3. V W A V V N M V
4. W W M N V W W M
5. K H K K M X Y K

C **Copy.**

Listening Practice 1

  A **Listen and circle.**

1. I ⬭T⬯ L

2. L H T

3. X A Y

4. F E H

5. W M K

6. N V X

7. H T L

8. A E I

9. F K Y

10. M N V

A **Listen.**

U C O Q

Listen and repeat.

B **Circle.**

1. U   C   O   (U)   V   C   (U)   (U)

2. C   C   O   Q   C   U   D   C

3. O   U   O   C   O   O   D   Q

4. Q   O   Q   D   Q   D   O   Q

C **Copy.**

U   U   U

C   C   C

O   O   O

Q   Q   Q

P R B D

A Listen.

P   R   B   D

Listen and repeat.

B Circle.

1. P   R   B   (P)   D   (P)   R   (P)

2. R   K   R   P   R   D   R   P

3. B   P   B   A   B   B   R   D

4. D   O   P   D   Q   O   D   D

C Copy.

P   P   P

R   R   R

B   B   B

D   D   D

A Listen.

S   G   J   Z

Listen and repeat.

B Circle.

1. S   Z   Ⓢ   G   Ⓢ   Q   Ⓢ   G
2. G   G   Q   S   G   D   Q   G
3. J   I   U   J   L   J   U   J
4. Z   S   Z   N   Z   X   Z   S

C Copy.

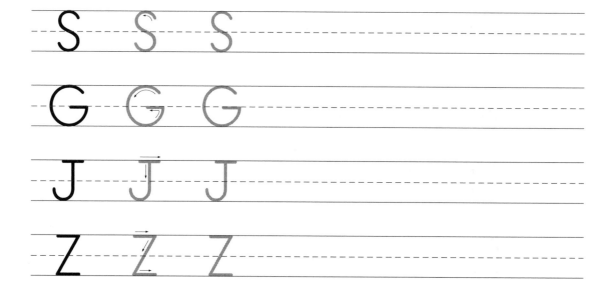

S   S   S

G   G   G

J   J   J

Z   Z   Z

Listening Practice 2

  A **Listen and circle.**

1. U   O   (Q)

2. C   Q   U

3. P   B   D

4. R   D   T

5. J   G   S

6. G   S   Z

7. O   D   G

8. S   C   R

9. Z   J   P

10. G   B   U

l t i j

 A Listen.

| l | t | i | j |

Listen and repeat.

B Circle.

1. l   t   (l)   f   (l)   b   (l)   k

2. t   t   f   l   k   t   f   t

3. i   j   i   l   i   j   i   f

4. j   j   i   q   j   g   j   y

C Copy.

V W X Z

 A **Listen.**

V   W   X   Z

Listen and repeat.

B **Circle.**

1. v   (v)   x   w   (v)   y   (v)   z

2. w   x   v   w   w   z   w   x

3. x   v   x   z   w   x   z   x

4. z   z   x   n   z   v   w   z

C **Copy.**

V   V   V

W   W   W

X   X   X

Z   Z   Z

🎧 **A** **Listen.**

o   c   a   e   s

Listen and repeat.

B **Circle.**

1. **o**   a   (o)   c   (o)   (o)   e   a

2. **c**   e   c   a   o   c   c   e

3. **a**   a   d   e   a   o   c   a

4. **e**   e   c   e   a   o   e   c

5. **s**   c   s   e   s   s   a   c

C **Copy.**

o o o

c c c

a a a

e e e

s s s

Listening Practice 3

  Listen and circle.

1.   l   (t)   j

2.   i   l   t

3.   s   w   z

4.   v   m   w

5.   s   e   a

6.   c   o   e

7.   v   c   t

8.   e   o   a

9.   x   j   c

10.   l   z   t

u r n h m

🎧 **A** **Listen.**

u r n h m

Listen and repeat.

B **Circle.**

1. **u**   m   (u)   n   o   (u)   (u)   r

2. **r**   r   n   u   m   u   r   r

3. **n**   m   u   n   n   h   u   n

4. **h**   h   n   u   h   w   h   p

5. **m**   n   m   b   d   m   h   m

C **Copy.**

u   u   u

r   r   r

n   n   n

h   h   h

m   m   m

b d p q

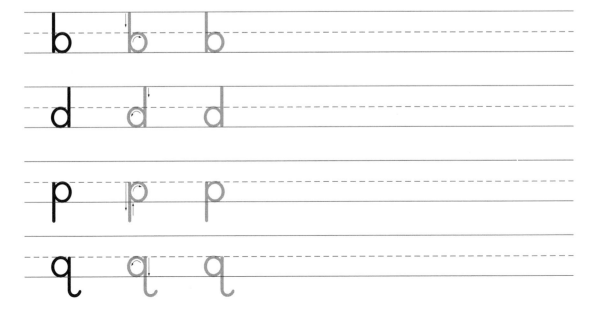

A Listen.

b   d   p   q

Listen and repeat.

B Circle.

1. **b**   d   h   ⓑ   ⓑ   p   ⓑ   d

2. **d**   b   d   a   d   b   b   d

3. **p**   g   p   p   q   y   p   j

4. **q**   g   q   p   q   p   q   y

C Copy.

b   b   b

d   d   d

p   p   p

q   q   q

y g f k

A Listen.

y   g   f   k

Listen and repeat.

B Circle.

1. y   g   (y)   (y)   j   q   (y)   v

2. g   g   q   g   g   q   j   y

3. f   f   f   t   t   h   f   k

4. k   k   h   x   k   l   f   k

C Copy.

y   y   y

g   g   g

f   f   f

k   k   k

Listening Practice 4

 A **Listen and circle.**

1. g (u) r

2. h m k

3. p d q

4. h b d

5. k l f

6. g j y

7. h f b

8. y m n

9. p b g

10. r g q

Uppercase and Lowercase Letters

 A **Listen.**

Aa   Bb   Cc   Dd

Listen and repeat.

 B **Listen and circle.**

1. B   C   (D)

2. D   A   C

3. c   b   a

4. b   a   d

C **Copy.**

Uppercase Letters   Lowercase Letters

1. A A A _____   a a a _____

2. B B B _____   b b b _____

3. C C C _____   c c c _____

4. D D D _____   d d d _____

Uppercase and Lowercase Letters

🎧 **A** **Listen.**

Ee   Ff   Gg   Hh

Listen and repeat.

🎧 **B** **Listen and circle.**

1. H   (G)   F

2. E   F   H

3. f   e   h

4. h   f   g

C **Copy.**

Uppercase Letters	Lowercase Letters
1. E E E _____	e e e _____
2. F F F _____	f f f _____
3. G G G _____	g g g _____
4. H H H _____	h h h _____

Uppercase and Lowercase Letters

 A **Listen.**

$$ Ii \quad Jj \quad Kk \quad Ll $$

Listen and repeat.

B **Listen and circle.**

1. (J) K L

2. L I K

3. k l i

4. i j l

C **Copy.**

Uppercase Letters   Lowercase Letters

1. I I I _____   i i i _____

2. J J J _____   j j j _____

3. K K K _____   k k k _____

4. L L L _____   l l l _____

Uppercase and Lowercase Letters

 A **Listen.**

Mm   Nn   Oo   Pp

Listen and repeat.

 B **Listen and circle.**

1. O   M   (P)

2. M   N   O

3. o   p   n

4. n   p   m

C **Copy.**

Uppercase Letters | Lowercase Letters

1. M M M _____   m m m _____

2. N N N _____   n n n _____

3. O O O _____   o o o _____

4. P P P _____   p p p _____

Uppercase and Lowercase Letters

🎧 **A** **Listen.**

Qq Rr Ss Tt Uu

Listen and repeat.

🎧 **B** **Listen and circle.**

1. (R) S Q

2. T R U

3. r u q

4. t r s

C **Copy.**

Uppercase Letters	Lowercase Letters
1. Q Q Q _____	q q q _____
2. R R R _____	r r r _____
3. S S S _____	s s s _____
4. T T T _____	t t t _____
5. U U U _____	u u u _____

Uppercase and Lowercase Letters

  A **Listen.**

V v　W w　X x　Y y　Z z

Listen and repeat.

  B **Listen and circle.**

1. V　Y　W

2. W　X　Z

3. y　z　x

4. w　v　y

C **Copy.**

Uppercase Letters	Lowercase Letters
1. V V V _____	v v v _____
2. W W W _____	w w w _____
3. X X X _____	x x x _____
4. Y Y Y _____	y y y _____
5. Z Z Z _____	z z z _____

Uppercase and Lowercase Letters

A **Match.**

_c_ 1. S   a. u

____ 2. C   b. o

____ 3. U   c. s

____ 4. O   d. c

B **Match.**

_e_ 1. I   a. v

____ 2. Y   b. k

____ 3. K   c. w

____ 4. W   d. y

____ 5. V   e. i

Uppercase and Lowercase Letters

A Circle the lowercase letter.

1. N   m   h   (n)
2. F   t   f   l
3. L   h   i   l
4. A   a   o   c

B Circle the lowercase letter.

1. H   h   n   d
2. R   n   r   k
3. E   e   o   c
4. G   q   p   g

C Circle the lowercase letter.

1. D   h   d   b
2. T   t   l   i
3. Q   g   j   q
4. B   b   h   d
5. R   n   m   r

Uppercase Letters in Words

A **Circle the letter.**

1. A (A)ND   CHAIR   TALL
2. B BLUE   BOY   NOTEBOOK
3. C CLASS   NICE   COPY
4. D DESK   DOOR   BOARD

B **Circle the letter.**

1. E EIGHT   PAPER   PEN
2. F FIVE   FIRST   FOUR
3. G GRACE   EIGHT   GO
4. H HI   PHONE   THREE

C **Circle the letter.**

1. I IS   NICE   THIS
2. J JAR   JOB   JOHNSON
3. K KEY   TAKE   TALK
4. L LAST   CLASS   CLOSE
5. M MY   MEET   NAME

Uppercase Letters in Words

A Circle the letter.

1. N   (N)O   NAME   ON
2. O   ONE   POINT   YOU
3. P   PEN   PARK   OPEN
4. Q   QUICK   QUIT   QUEEN

B Circle the letter.

1. R   RED   MARIA   YOUR
2. S   STREET   CARLOS   DESK
3. T   TWO   WHAT   TIEN
4. U   USA   BLUE   PUT

C Circle the letter.

1. V   VERY   FIVE   LIVE
2. W   WALK   WHAT   WEEK
3. X   SIX   EXIT   TAXI
4. Y   YES   YOUR   SAY
5. Z   ZERO   SIZE   ZIP CODE

Lowercase Letters in Words

A Circle the letter.

1. **a** (a)n d   C h i n a   t a l l

2. **b** b l u e   n u m b e r   b o y

3. **c** c o p y   c h a i r   n i c e

4. **d** d o   d o o r   a n d

B Circle the letter.

1. **e** e m a i l   p a p e r   p e n

2. **f** f i v e   f i r s t   o f

3. **g** g o   e i g h t   w a l k i n g

4. **h** h e l l o   p h o n e   w h a t

C Circle the letter.

1. **i** i s   n i c e   h i

2. **j** j u m p   j o b   j a c k e t

3. **k** t a l k   b o o k   k i t c h e n

4. **l** l a s t   c l a s s   l u n c h

Lowercase Letters in Words

A Circle the letter.

1. **m** (m)y   m e e t   n a m e
2. **n** n o   n a m e   o n
3. **o** o n e   y o u r   y o u
4. **p** p e n   c o p y   o p e n
5. **q** q u i c k   q u i t   q u a r t e r

B Circle the letter.

1. **r** r e d   r o o m   y o u r
2. **s** s t o p   s p e a k   d e s k
3. **t** t w o   w h a t   t h r e e
4. **u** u p   y o u   p u t

C Circle the letter.

1. **v** s e v e n   f i v e   l i v e
2. **w** w r i t e   b r o w n   w e e k
3. **x** t a x i   s i x   M e x i c o
4. **y** y e s   y o u r   s a y
5. **z** z e r o   s i z e   z i p   c o d e

Numbers 0–5

A Listen.

0	1	2
zero	one	two
3	4	5
three	four	five

Listen and repeat.

B Copy.

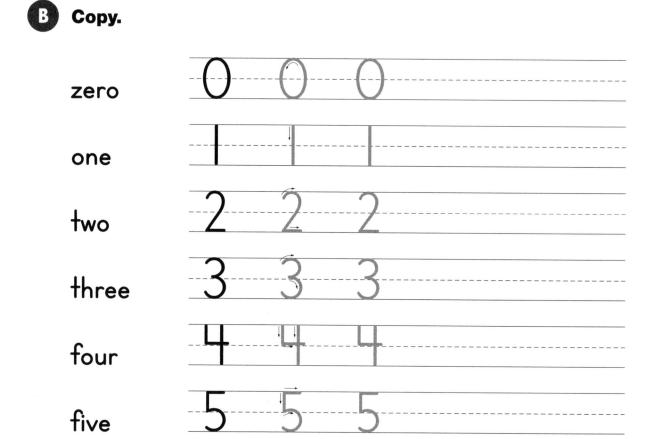

zero	O O O
one	1 1 1
two	2 2 2
three	3 3 3
four	4 4 4
five	5 5 5

A **Listen.**

6	7	8
six	seven	eight

9	10
nine	ten

Listen and repeat.

B **Copy.**

six   6 6 6

seven   7 7 7

eight   8 8 8

nine   9 9 9

ten   10 10 10

Number Practice

A Circle.

1. 7

2. 5

3. 2

4. 4

5. 10

B Match.

_c_ 1. 3   a.

___ 2. 9   b.

___ 3. 1   c.

___ 4. 7   d.

___ 5. 4   e.

Number Practice

A Circle.

1. 5
   (2)
   7

2. 0
   1   zero
   2

3. 3
   4
   5

4. 7
   8   seven
   9

5. 1
   2
   3

6. 8
   9
   10

7. 6
   7   eight
   8

8. 1
   2
   3

9. 8
   9   ten
   10

10. 2
    3
    4

Section One

Number Practice

A Circle.

1. 8
   (3)
   5

2. 2
   4   one
   1

3. 9
   8
   7

4. 5
   6   five
   10

5. 4
   9
   10

Letter Review

A Listen.

A B C D E F G H I J K L M

Listen and repeat.

B Write.

A B C D _ F _ H I J _ L _

C Listen.

a b c d e f g h i j k l m

Listen and repeat.

D Write.

a b c _ _ f g _ i _ k l m

E Listen and circle.

1. (G) E B C

2. J C G B

3. a h f e

4. m e i l

Letter Review

 A Listen.

NOPQRSTUVWXYZ

Listen and repeat.

B Write.

N   O   P   Q   __   __   T   __   V   __   X   __   Z

 C Listen.

n o p q r s t u v w x y z

Listen and repeat.

D Write.

n   o   __   __   __   s   __   u   v   __   __   y   __

 E Listen and circle.

1.   X   K   S   Ⓩ

2.   Q   O   C   G

3.   w   s   z   y

4.   u   v   m   w

Number Review

🎧 **A** **Listen.**

0 1 2 3 4 5 6 7 8 9 10

Listen and repeat.

B **Write.**

_0_   1   __   3   4   __   __   7   __   9   __

🎧 **C** **Listen and circle.**

1.   5   0   1   4   2

2.   8   10   6   9   7

D **Copy.**

1 _1_   3 __   2 __

4 __   7 __   8 __

6 __   5 __   9 __

Section 2　Phonics Practice

Taking Off
Beginning English

Susan Hancock Fesler ★ Christy M. Newman

Section Two

39

Consonants *b* and *d*

  A **Listen.**

book

desk

Listen and repeat.

  B **Listen.**

bus   **bat**   **dish**   **door**

Listen and repeat.

  C **Listen and circle.**

1. ban   (Dan)   2. bug   dug   3. big   dig

4. bay   day   5. Ben   den   6. bark   dark

  D **Listen and write *b* or *d*.**

1. b ag   2. ___esk   3. ___ook

4. ___ay   5. ___oor   6. ___ox

Listen and repeat.

Section Two

Consonants *p* and *t*

  A **Listen.**

pan

10
ten

Listen and repeat.

  B **Listen.**

pants

pie

tooth

tub

Listen and repeat.

  C **Listen and circle.**

1. pie (tie)   2. pen   ten   3. pin   tin

4. pick   tick   5. pan   tan   6. pail   tail

 D **Listen and write *p* or *t*.**

1. p ink   2. ___en   3. ___alk

4. ___ot   5. ___ay   6. ___ug

Listen and repeat.

Listening Practice   *b*, *d*, *p*, and *t*

 A Listen and circle *b*, *d*, *p*, or *t*.

1.

   (b) d p t

2.

   b d p t

3. **10**

   b d p t

4.

   b d p t

5.

   b d p t

6.

   b d p t

7.

   b d p t

8.

   b d p t

 B Listen and write *b*, *d*, *p*, or *t*.

1. _p_ie   2. ___ub   3. ___ig   4. ___at

5. ___ell   6. ___ish   7. ___ed   8. ___ell

Listen and repeat.

Consonants *f* and *h*

 A **Listen.**

feet

hand

Listen and repeat.

 B **Listen.**

fan   fish   hat   hen

Listen and repeat.

 C **Listen and circle.**

1. fat   (hat)   2. fit   hit   3. fall   hall

4. fair   hair   5. fear   here   6. fill   hill

 D **Listen and write *f* or *h*.**

1. __h__e   2. ___ive   3. ___ix

4. ___ello   5. ___er   6. ___ather

Listen and repeat.

Consonants *g* and *j*

 A **Listen.**

girl

jay

Listen and repeat.

 B **Listen.**

goat   gas   jug   jacket

Listen and repeat.

 C **Listen and circle.**

1. (go)   Joe   2. gay   jay   3. got   jot

4. gone   John   5. gob   job   6. get   jet

 D **Listen and write *g* or *j*.**

1. _g_ap   2. ___as   3. ___ar

4. ___eans   5. ___ame   6. ___uice

Listen and repeat.

A Listen and circle *f, g, h,* or *j.*

1.

f (g) h j

2.

f g h j

3.

f g h j

4.

f g h j

5.

f g h j

6.

f g h j

7.

f g h j

8.

f g h j

  B Listen and write *f, g, h,* or *j.*

1. h_at   2. ___eep   3. ___irst   4. ___irl

5. ___ug   6. ___et   7. ___and   8. ___ish

Listen and repeat.

Consonants *l* and *r*

  A **Listen.**

leg

rug

Listen and repeat.

  B **Listen.**

lamp   lock   rake   rose

Listen and repeat.

  C **Listen and circle.**

1. (lip)   rip   2. lay   ray   3. lap   rap

4. lake   rake   5. light right 6. load   road

 D **Listen and write *l* or *r*.**

1. r̲ead   2. ___and   3. ___un

4. ___ook   5. ___ist   6. ___ed

Listen and repeat.

Consonants *m* and *n*

 A **Listen.**

man

nose

Listen and repeat.

 B **Listen.**

map

mug

9

nine

nest

Listen and repeat.

 C **Listen and circle.**

1. (map)   nap   2. mine   nine   3. mail   nail

4. met   net   5. moon   noon   6. meet   neat

 D **Listen and write *m* or *n*.**

1. _n_ot   2. ___at   3. ___eck

4. ___ay   5. ___ear   6. ___ake

Listen and repeat.

Listening Practice   *l, m, n,* and *r*

🎧 **A** **Listen and circle *l, m, n,* or *r*.**

1.

   l   m   n   (r)

2.

   l   m   n   r

3.

   l   m   n   r

4. **9**

   l   m   n   r

5.

   l   m   n   r

6.

   l   m   n   r

7.

   l   m   n   r

8.

   l   m   n   r

🎧 **B** **Listen and write *l, m, n,* or *r*.**

1. _m_ an   2. ___oom   3. ___ext   4. ___ose

5. ___ilk   6. ___ug   7. ___unch   8. ___arge

Listen and repeat.

Section Two

Consonants *k* and *qu*

 A **Listen.**

kite

quilt

Listen and repeat.

 B **Listen.**

key   kilt   queen   quarter

Listen and repeat.

 C **Listen and circle.**

1. (kid)   quid   2. kit   quit   3. kale   quail

4. kilt   quilt   5. kick   quick   6. kite   quite

 D **Listen and write *k* or *qu*.**

1. _k_iss   2. ___it   3. ___ey

4. ___ick   5. ___art   6. ___eep

Listen and repeat.

Consonants *v* and *w*

  A **Listen.**

van

watch

Listen and repeat.

  B **Listen.**

vest   violin   wiper   window

Listen and repeat.

  C **Listen and circle.**

1. (vet)   wet   2. V   we   3. vent   went

4. vale   wail   5. vest   west   6. vow   wow

 D **Listen and write *v* or *w*.**

1. w eek   2. ___ery   3. ___ork

4. ___et   5. ___isit   6. ___at

Listen and repeat.

Section Two

Listening Practice *k, qu, v,* and *w*

  A Listen and circle *k, qu, v,* or *w.*

1.

k (qu) v w

2.

k qu v w

3.

k qu v w

4.

k qu v w

5.

k qu v w

6.

k qu v w

7.

k qu v w

8.

k qu v w

 B Listen and write *k, qu, v,* or *w.*

1. __v__an   2. __alk   3. __iet   4. __it

5. __est   6. __ick   7. __ite   8. __ant

Listen and repeat.

51

Consonants *x* and *y*

 A **Listen.**

fox

yarn

Listen and repeat.

 B **Listen.**

6

six

box

yo-yo

yard

Listen and repeat.

 C **Listen and write *x*.**

1. <u>x</u>-ray

2. ta__i

3. fi__

Listen and repeat.

 D **Listen and write *y*.**

1. <u>y</u>ell

2. __ak

3. __ardstick

Listen and repeat.

Section Two

Consonants *s* and *z*

  A Listen.

sink

zipper

Listen and repeat.

  B Listen.

sun

6

six

zip code

zebra

Listen and repeat.

  C Listen and circle.

1. Sue (zoo)   2. sip   zip   3. sag   zag

4. sink   zinc   5. sing   zing   6. sipper   zipper

  D Listen and write *s* or *z.*

1. _s_ ofa   2. ___it   3. ___oom

4. ___one   5. ___ister   6. ___ero

Listen and repeat.

Consonants *c*

  A **Listen.**

cap   circle

Listen and repeat.

  B **Listen.**

cat   corn   city   cent

Listen and repeat.

  C **Listen and write c.**

1. _c_ an   2. ___ook   3. ___ity

4. ___ircle   5. ___ube   6. ___ell

Listen and repeat.

Listening Practice   *c, s, x, y,* and *z*

🎧 **A** Listen and circle *c, s, x, y,* or *z.*

1.

c s (x) y z

2.

c s x y z

3.

c s x y z

4.

c s x y z

5.

c s x y z

6.
0
c s x y z

7.

c s x y z

8.

c s x y z

9.

10028
c s x y z

10.

c s x y z

🎧 **B** Listen and write *c, s, x, y,* or *z.*

1. mi<u>x</u>   2. ___our   3. ___ay   4. ___old

5. ___ip   6. ne___t   7. ___ent   8. ___oung

Short Vowels *a*

 A **Listen.**

ant

man

pan

cap

Listen and repeat.

 B **Listen and ✔ check.**

1. ___

2. ✔

3. ___

10

4. ___

5. ___

6. ___

 C **Listen and write *a*.**

1. <u>a</u>m   2. l__st   3. cl__ss   4. __ddress

Listen and repeat.

Short Vowels *e*

  A **Listen.**

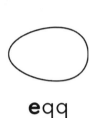   

egg   pen   desk   leg

Listen and repeat.

  B **Listen and ✔ check.**

   **7**   **10**

1. ___   2. ✔___   3. ___

4. ___   5. ___   6. ___

  C **Listen and write e.**

1. _e_nd   2. ___xit   3. m___n   4. c___ll

Listen and repeat.

Listening Practice   Short *a* and *e*

 A **Listen and circle *a* or *e*.**

1.

   (a) e

2.

   a e

3.

   a e

4.

   a e

 B **Listen and circle.**

1. and   (end)   2. pan   pen

3. Dan   den   4. man   men

5. bag   beg   6. tax   Tex

7. ham   hem   8. mat   met

 C **Listen and write *a* or *e*.**

1. r_e_d   2. ___nd   3. b___ll

4. t___n   5. m___n   6. p___ck

Listen and repeat.

Short Vowels *i*

 A **Listen.**

dish   sit   pill   **6**

six

Listen and repeat.

 B **Listen and ✔ check.**

1. ✔   2. ___   3. ___

4. ___   5. ___   6. ___

 C **Listen and write *i*.**

1. _i_t   2. __n   3. h__s   4. l__st

Listen and repeat.

Section Two

59

Short Vowels *o*

  A **Listen.**

  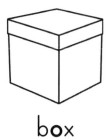 

sock   cot   box   clock

Listen and repeat.

 B **Listen and ✔ check.**

1. ✔   2. ___   3. ___

4. ___   5. ___   6. ___

C **Listen and write *o*.**

1. o n   2. h __ t   3. j __ b   4. st __ p

Listen and repeat.

Short Vowels *u*

  A Listen.

bus	tub	nut	rug

Listen and repeat.

  B Listen and ✔ check.

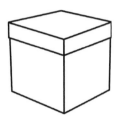  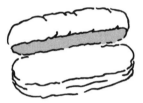

1. ___   2. ✔   3. ___

4. ___   5. ___   6. ___

  C Listen and write *u*.

1. <u>u</u> s   2. ___ p   3. s___n   4. l___nch

Listen and repeat.

Listening Practice Short *i*, *o*, and *u*

 A Listen and circle *i*, *o*, or *u*.

1.

   i o (u)

2.

   i o u

3.

   i o u

4.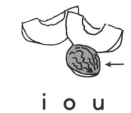

   i o u

5.

   i o u

6.

   i o u

 B Listen and circle.

1. in   (on)   2. fin   fun   3. cot   cut

4. fix   fox   5. rib   rub   6. not   nut

7. sick   sock   8. big   bug   9. doll   dull

 C Listen and write *i*, *o*, or *u*.

1. r_o_ck   2. p__t   3. b__g   4. b__s

5. h__g   6. __p   7. f__x   8. cl__ck

Listen and repeat.

Listening Practice   Short *a*, *e*, *i*, *o*, and *u*

A Listen and write *a*, *e*, *i*, *o*, or *u*.

1.

p_a_nts

2.

g__ft

3.

p__t

4.

d__sk

5.

b__ll

6.

t__b

7.

b__s

8.
b__x

9.

j__cket

10.

l__nch

11.

12

tw__lve

12.

n__ckel

Long Vowels *a*, *e*, and *i*

	Long *a*		
raining	**ay**	**a-e**	**ai**
	day	age	aid
	say	name	raining
	playing	safety	waiter

	Long *e*			
eat	**e**	**ee**	**ea**	**y**
	be	see	eat	baby
	he	three	beans	family
	she	between	reading	twenty

	Long *i*			
ice	**i-e**	**ie**	**igh**	**y**
	ice	lie	high	cry
	five	pie	right	July
	write	tie	lighter	flying

Long Vowels *o* and *u*

	Long *o*			
	o	**o-e**	**oa**	**ow**
sofa	go no sofa	close nose stove	coat soap toast	grow slowly snowing

	Long *u*			
	u-e	**ui**	**ue**	**ou**
cube	use cube computer	fruit juice suit	Sue blue clue	you soup group

Section 3   Support Exercises for Student Book

🎧 **A** Listen.

F f   L l   N n

Listen and repeat.

B Write.

1. F f   F IRST   f our
2. L l   C__OSE   __isten
3. N n   __AME   __ice

C Circle.

1. FIRST   (FIRST)   FIVE   FOUR
2. LAST   LIST   LEFT   LAST
3. **name**   nine   name   meet
4. **notebook**   book   computer   notebook

1. FIRST   (LAST)   NAME

2. first   last   name

3. First   Last   Name

E **Circle _NAME_ and _name_.**

IDENTIFICATION FORM

(NAME:)

Grace   Lee

FIRST NAME   LAST NAME

IDENTIFICATION FORM

Write your name:

Lee   Grace

last name   first name

F **Write. Say the word.**

1. **F or f**   F IRST   __irst   __IRST

2. **L or l**   __AST   __ast   __AST

3. **N or n**   __ame   __AME   __ame

G **Listen.**

1.

student

2.

teacher

3.

book

4.

notebook

5.

pen

6.

backpack

Listen and repeat.

H **Circle. Say the word.**

1. **backpack**   book   (backpack)   student

2. **book**   student   pen   book

3. **notebook**   notebook   student   teacher

4. **pen**   backpack   notebook   pen

I Write.

1.    book

2.    _____

3.    _____

4.    _____

J Write.

1.

   Tien Lam

   <u>Lam</u>
   last name

   _____
   first name

2.

   Leo Danov

   _____
   LAST NAME

   _____
   FIRST NAME

Listen and repeat.

I am = I'm

It is = It's

What is = What's

L **Match.**

___b___ 1. I'm   a. What is

_____ 2. It's   b. I am

_____ 3. What's   c. It is

M **Write.**

1. I _a m_ from China.

2. I'___ from Mexico.

3. W___ ___t i___ this?

4. It'___ a backpack.

5. ___ ___ ___ ___'s this?

6. ___ ___ is a notebook.

N **Read.**

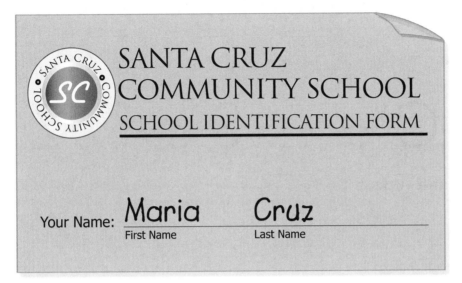

SANTA CRUZ
COMMUNITY SCHOOL
SCHOOL IDENTIFICATION FORM

Your Name: **Maria**   **Cruz**
First Name   Last Name

O **Write about you.**

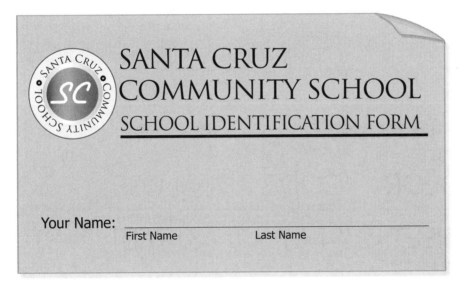

SANTA CRUZ
COMMUNITY SCHOOL
SCHOOL IDENTIFICATION FORM

Your Name: _____
First Name   Last Name

IDENTIFICATION FORM

WRITE YOUR NAME:

LAST NAME   FIRST NAME

A **Listen.**

C c   S s   Z z

Listen and repeat.

B **Write.**

1. C c   _C_ITY   _c_ountry

2. S s   __TREET   __ix

3. Z z   __ERO   __oo

C **Circle. Say the word.**

1. COLOR   CODE   CLOSE   (COLOR)

2. STREET   STAY   STREET   STOP

3. **zip**   zip   sip   zap

4. **zero**   zone   nose   zero

D Listen and circle.

1. (state) street sixteen

2. city zip six

3. zip city dress

E Circle *CITY* and *City*.

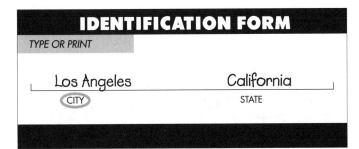

IDENTIFICATION FORM

TYPE OR PRINT

Los Angeles California
(CITY) STATE

Welcome to New York City

F Circle *STATE* and *State*.

IDENTIFICATION FORM

PLEASE WRITE YOUR NAME, ADDRESS, CITY, AND STATE

Leo V. Danov
NAME

1710 Sunset Street
ADDRESS

Los Angeles CA
CITY STATE

CALIFORNIA
000 000
The Golden State

1.
single

2.
married

3.
divorced

4.
widowed

Listen and repeat.

H ✔**Check.**

	Single	Married	Divorced	Widowed
1.	✔			
2.				
3.				
4.				

I **Match.**

address

city

name

state

zip code

Maria Cruz
20 Paper Street
Los Angeles, California 90011

J **Write.**

10 Pen Street   ~~Paul S. Lemat~~   Los Angeles
90015   CA

IDENTIFICATION FORM

TYPE OR PRINT

Lemat

LAST NAME

Paul

FIRST NAME

S.

MI

ADDRESS   CITY   STATE   ZIP CODE

🎧 **K** **Listen.**

AM, IS, ARE		
I	**am**	from Somalia.
He	**is**	from Somalia.
She	**is**	from Somalia.
They	**are**	from Somalia.

Listen and repeat.

L **Match.**

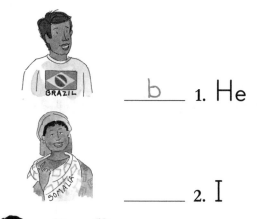

_b_ 1. He   a. are from China.

_____ 2. I   b. is from Brazil.

_____ 3. They   c. am from Somalia.

M **Read.**

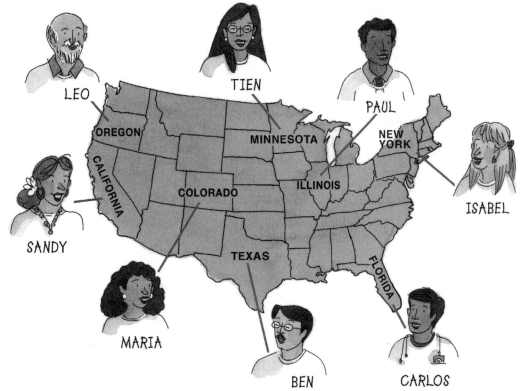

N **Write the states.**

A–M	N–Z
California	New York

O **Write your state.**

I am in _____.

A **Listen.**

H h   M m   Y y

Listen and repeat.

B **Write.**

1. H h   H ER   h is

2. M m   __OTHER   fa__ily

3. Y y   __OUNG   prett__

C **Circle. Say the word.**

1. HIS   HIS   HIT   HIM

2. MOTHER   MISTER   MOTHER   MATTER

3. your   year   your   yes

4. husband   husband   how   help

🎧 **D** **Listen and circle.**

1. you   (yes)   years
2. father   family   fine
3. mother   Maria   middle-aged

E **Match.**

__d__ 1. MOTHER   a. father

____ 2. FAMILY   b. daughter

____ 3. DAUGHTER   c. family

____ 4. FATHER   d. mother

F **Read.**

Children

Son   Father   Mother   Daughter

Family

G ✔ Check.

1. _____ father   ✔ family

2. _____ children   _____ son

H Circle.

1.

    son   (daughter)

2.

    father   son

3.

    mother   father

4.

    father   son

Listen.

My name is Mary.

My mother's name is Yoko.

My father's name is Harry.

My brother's name is Mike.

This is my family.

Mary

Listen and repeat.

J Write. Say the sentence.

1. My name is <u>M</u>ary.

2. My mother's name is ___oko.

3. My father's name is ___arry.

4. My brother's name is ___ike.

5. T___is is ___y fa___il___.

K Write about you.

1. My mother's name is _____.

2. My father's name is _____.

🎧 **L** **Listen.**

MY, YOUR, HIS, HER

My name is Sandy.

Your name is Leo.

His name is Paul.

Her name is Isabel.

Listen and repeat.

M **Circle.**

1. My   Ms.   (My)   Mr.
2. YOUR   YARN   YOU   YOUR
3. his   his   hit   ham
4. Her   Has   Hair   Her

N **Write.**

1. <u>M</u>y name is Sandy.

2. ___ou___ name is Leo.

3. H___ ___ name is Paul.

4. ___ ___ ___ name is Isabel.

O Read.

Her Relatives

P Write.

1. Juma and Ubah are _____married_____.
   (married/students)

2. Hindi is Nadira's _____.
   (mother/father)

3. Ubah is Nadira's _____.
   (son/grandmother)

4. Juma, Ubah, Hindi, and Nadira

   are _____.
   (relatives/brothers)

Q Write about you.

My Relatives

Relative	Name
grandmother	
grandfather	
mother	
father	

🎧 **A** Listen.

B b   D d   R r

Listen and repeat.

B Write.

1. B b   <u>B</u>EDROOM   <u>b</u>ed

2. D d   __RESSER   __esk

3. R r   __OOM   __ug

C Circle. Say the word.

1. BED   ⬭BED⬭   BAD   DAB

2. DOOR   ROOM   DOOR   DO

3. **read**   red   dear   read

4. **dresser**   dress   dresser   dresses

D **Match.**

___c___ 1. BED   a. rug

_____ 2. DOOR   b. tub

_____ 3. BEDROOM   c. bed

_____ 4. RUG   d. door

_____ 5. TUB   e. bedroom

E **Listen.**

1.
bathroom

2.
bed

3.
tub

4.
dining room

5.
dresser

6.
window

7.
rug

8.
refrigerator

9.
shower

Listen and repeat.

F ✔ **Check.**

1.

_____ tub
__✔__ bed

2.

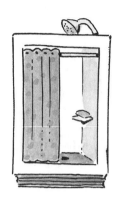

_____ rug
_____ shower

3.

_____ bathroom
_____ dining room

4.

_____ dresser
_____ window

5.

_____ tub
_____ shower

6.

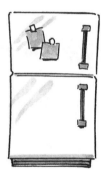

_____ refrigerator
_____ lamp

G **Write *b*, *d*, or *r*. Say the word.**

1. _r_ug

2. ___oor

3. ___resser

4. ___ath___oom

5. ___ef___ige___ato___

🎧 **H** **Listen and circle.**

1. bedroom   (bathroom)
2. dining room   living room
3. living room   bedroom
4. sink   tub
5. fireplace   closet

I ✔ **Check.**

	Kitchen	Living Room	Bedroom	Bathroom
1. bed			✔	
2. dresser				
3. refrigerator				
4. rug				
5. sofa				
6. tub				

🎧 **J** **Listen.**

| SINGULAR AND PLURAL NOUNS ||
Singular	Plural
one sofa	two sofas
one shower	four showers

Listen and repeat.

K ✔ **Check.**

1.

_____ 1 window
✔ 4 windows

2.

_____ 1 tub
_____ 5 tubs

3.

_____ 1 bed
_____ 2 beds

4.

_____ 1 rug
_____ 3 rugs

L **Read.**

Tien's Apartment

Her building

Her apartment

Her balcony

M **Write.**

1. Tien is at _____home_____ .
   (school/home)

2. Her apartment building has
   _____(6/16)_____ floors.

3. Her apartment is number
   _____(305/503)_____ .

4. It has a __(balcony/dining room)__ .

A Listen.

A a   E e   T t

Listen and repeat.

B Write.

1. A a   <u>A</u>PRIL   Mond<u>a</u>y
2. E e   __NGLISH   r__ad
3. T t   __UESDAY   __ime

C Circle.

1. APRIL   APPLE   (APRIL)   PAPER
2. EVERY   EVERY   EVER   NEVER
3. Thursday   Thursday   Thirsty   Tuesday
4. time   tame   time   mite

D **Match.**

___d___ 1. SUNDAY

_____ 2. MONDAY

_____ 3. TUESDAY

_____ 4. WEDNESDAY

_____ 5. THURSDAY

_____ 6. FRIDAY

_____ 7. SATURDAY

a. Friday

b. Monday

c. Saturday

d. Sunday

e. Thursday

f. Tuesday

g. Wednesday

E **Listen and circle.**

1. Sunday   (Tuesday)

2. Sunday   Monday

3. Saturday   Thursday

4. Monday   Friday

5. Saturday   Wednesday

6. Tuesday   Thursday

F **Match.**

___f___ 1. January   a. Apr.

_____ 2. February   b. Jun.

_____ 3. March   c. Feb.

_____ 4. April   d. May

_____ 5. May   e. Mar.

_____ 6. June   f̶. Jan.

G **Match.**

___b___ 1. July   a. Oct.

_____ 2. August   b̶. Jul.

_____ 3. September   c. Aug.

_____ 4. October   d. Nov.

_____ 5. November   e. Sept.

_____ 6. December   f. Dec.

H ✔**Check.**

	Day	Month
1. August		✔
2. Wednesday		
3. Thursday		
4. October		
5. July		
6. Saturday		

I **Circle the month.**

Identification Card

Name: Tien Lam

Date of Birth: (April) 4, 1986

Tony's Movie Rentals

Nadira Shaheen

Expires: Nov. 1, 2020

🎧 **J** **Listen.**

SIMPLE PRESENT TENSE	
I	walk.
We	walk.
You	walk.
They	walk.
He	walk**s**.
She	walk**s**.

Listen and repeat.

K **Write.**

listen

1. He ___listens___ to music every day.

swim

2. I _____ every day.

read

3. She _____ every day.

talk

4. We _____ on the phone every day.

L **Read.**

Birthday Party for
Isabel
She is 21!
Saturday, May 17 at 5 P.M.
at Ben and Grace's house

M **Write.**

1. It is a birthday party for ___Isabel___.
   (Isabel / Ben)

2. Isabel is _____.
   (17 / 21)

3. The party is on _____.
   (Saturday / Sunday)

4. The party is in _____.
   (March / May)

N **Write about you.**

My birthday is in _____.

A Listen.

J j   K k   Q q

Listen and repeat.

B Write.

1. J j   J UNE   j acket

2. K k   CLER___   snea___ers

3. Q q   ___UICK   ___uarter

C Circle. Say the word.

1. JACKET   JANUARY   TICKET   (JACKET)

2. SOCK   SICK   SOCK   SACK

3. quilt   quit   queen   quilt

4. job   jacket   job   jog

D **Listen.**

1.
dress

2.
sweater

3.
shoes

4.
suit

5.
shirt

6.
pants

7.
jacket

8.
watch

Listen and repeat.

E **Match.**

<u> c </u> 1.   **a.** jacket

_____ 2.   **b.** dress

_____ 3.   <s>c.</s> pants

_____ 4.   **d.** shirt

F Circle. Say the word.

1.

(sweater)   blouse

2.

shoes   pants

3.

suit   shirt

4.

watch   jacket

🎧 **G** Listen.

1.

a penny   1¢

2.

a nickel   5¢

3.

a dime   10¢

4.

a quarter   25¢

5.

a dollar $1.00

6.

five dollars $5.00

Listen and repeat.

H Circle.

1.   0¢   ⟨40¢⟩   45¢

2. $1.25 $1.50 $2.25

3.  $4.20 $2.10 $2.40

I Match.

_b_ 1.   a. $18.00

____ 2.   b. $8.25

____ 3.   c. $1.59

🎧 **J** **Listen.**

ADJECTIVES AND NOUNS			
Adjectives	small	medium	large
Nouns	shirt	shirt	shirt
Adjectives and Nouns	a small shirt	a medium shirt	a large shirt

Listen and repeat.

K ✔**Check.**

				small	medium	large
1.					✔	
2.						
3.						

L **Read.**

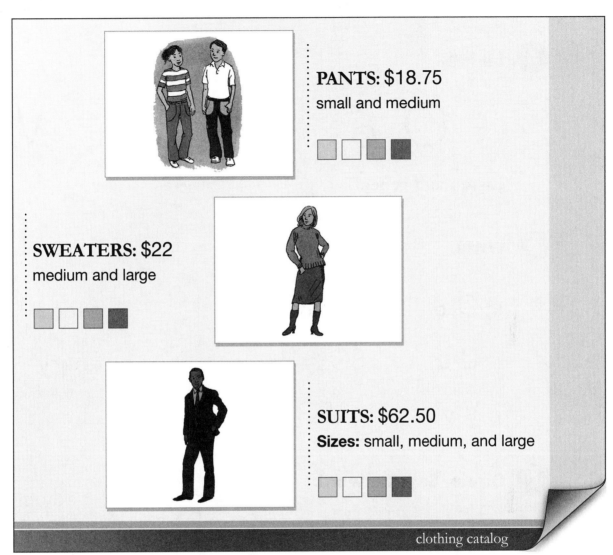

PANTS: $18.75
small and medium

SWEATERS: $22
medium and large

SUITS: $62.50
Sizes: small, medium, and large

clothing catalog

M **Write.**

1. ___Pants___ are $18.75.

2. _____ are $62.50.

3. Two sweaters are _____.

N **Write about you.**

I want to buy _____.

A   **Listen.**

O o   U u   V v

Listen and repeat.

B   **Write.**

1. O o   _O_ NION   ___range
2. U u   SO__P   h___ngry
3. V v   ___EGETABLE   ha__e

C   **Circle. Say the word.**

1. ORDER   OPEN   OVER   (ORDER)
2. BUTTER   BETTER   BUTTER   BATTER
3. have   have   heavy   hive
4. oil   old   oil   olive

D **Write the letter. Say the word.**

1. O or o   _O_RANGE   p__tat__es
2. U or u   j__ice   FR__IT
3. V or v   HA__E   __egetable

E **Match.**

___c___ 1. butter   a. CARROTS

_____ 2. carrots   b. ORANGES

_____ 3. oranges   c. BUTTER

F **Listen.**

1.
potatoes

2.
apples

3.
beef

4.
chicken

5.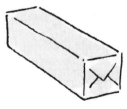
butter

6. carrots

Listen and repeat.

G Write the number.

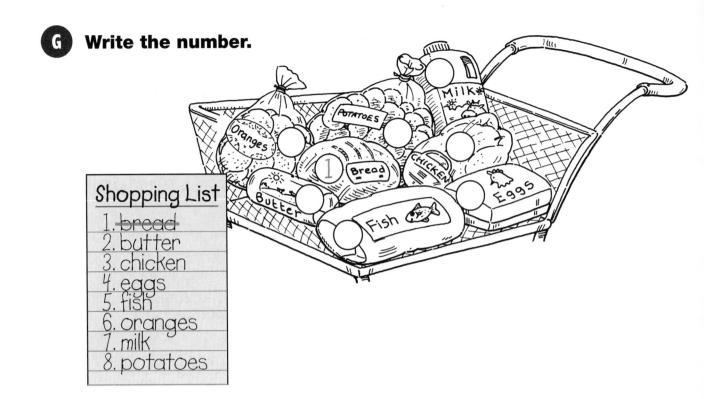

Shopping List
1. ~~bread~~
2. butter
3. chicken
4. eggs
5. fish
6. oranges
7. milk
8. potatoes

H Match.

____d____ 1.

a. bread

_____ 2.

b. cake

_____ 3.

c. ice cream

_____ 4.

~~d.~~ eggs

_____ 5.

e. milk

🎧 **I** **Listen and circle.**

1. (chicken)   lunch

2. cake   bread

3. juice   milk

4. apples   bananas

J **Read.**

Aisle 1	Aisle 2	Aisle 3
milk butter eggs	carrots apples potatoes	chicken beef fish

K **Look at Activity J. Circle the aisle.**

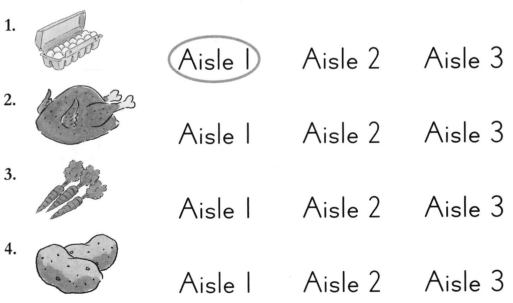

1. (Aisle 1)   Aisle 2   Aisle 3

2. Aisle 1   Aisle 2   Aisle 3

3. Aisle 1   Aisle 2   Aisle 3

4. Aisle 1   Aisle 2   Aisle 3

 **L** **Listen.**

COUNT NOUNS	
Singular	Plural (-s)
a carrot one carrot 	carrot**s** 

Listen and repeat.

M **Write.**

1. one apple <u>apples</u>

2. a chicken _____

3. one orange _____

4. a cake   _____

N Read.

O Write a shopping list.

1.

2.

3.

4.

juice

🎧 **A** **Listen.**

I i   W w

Listen and repeat.

B **Write.**

1. I i   <u>I</u>T'S   l__ke   spr__ng

2. W w   __EATHER   __indy   __alk

C **Circle. Say the word.**

1. I'M   IT'S   IN   (I'M)

2. WALK   WAIT   WALK   WORK

3. in   in   is   it

4. windy   winter   window   windy

D **Listen.**

1.

It's sunny.

2.
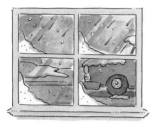
It's snowing.

3.

It's raining.

4.

It's windy.

Listen and repeat.

E **Match.**

___b___ 1.

a. It's windy.

_____ 2.

b. It's snowing.

_____ 3.

c. It's sunny.

_____ 4.

d. It's raining.

F **Read.**

1.
walking

2.
swimming

3.
playing soccer

4.
cooking

5.
watching TV

6.
listening to music

G **Match.**

___C___ 1.

a. watching TV

_____ 2.

b. playing soccer

_____ 3.

c. swimming

_____ 4.

d. walking

1. Nad_i_ra likes _w_alking and read_i_ng.

2. My name __s Isabel. I like s__imming.

3. Paul l__kes play__ng soccer.

4. Leo likes cook__ng and __atching TV.

5. T__en likes __atching TV and __alking, too.

6. Carlos l__kes l__sten__ng to mus__c.

I **Look at Activity H. Complete.**

1. Nadira likes ___walking___ and reading.

2. Isabel likes _____.

3. Paul likes _____ soccer.

4. Leo likes _____ and _____ TV.

5. Tien likes _____ TV and

   _____, too.

6. Carlos likes _____ to music.

 **Listen.**

PRESENT CONTINUOUS TENSE

I	am	eating.
He	is	eating.
She	is	eating.
We	are	eating.
You	are	eating.
They	are	eating.

Listen and repeat.

K **Write _am_, _is_, or _are_.**

1. She _____is_____ reading.

2. They _____ walking.

3. I _____ cooking.

4. He _____ talking.

L Read.

M Write.

snow

1. It _____is snowing_____ outside.

eat

2. They _____ lunch.

read

3. Leo _____ the newspaper.

work

4. Tien _____ on the computer.

talk

5. Nadira _____ on her cell phone.

N Write about you.

I am _____.

Where's the post office?

Student Book
Pages
138–153

A Listen.

G g   P p   X x

Listen and repeat.

B Write.

1. G g   _G_O   ___roup

2. P p   ___OST OFFICE   ___olice

3. X x   E___CUSE ME   ne___t

C Circle.

1. GOING   GONG   GOING   GONE

2. PLAY   PAL   PLAY   PAY

3. taxi   tax   taxi   taxing

4. park   part   park   pick

D **Write the letter. Say the words.**

1. **G** or **g**   _G_AS STATION   dru__store
2. **P** or **p**   hos__ital   SU__ERMARKET
3. **X** or **x**   E__CUSE ME   e__it

E **Listen.**

Listen and repeat.

F **Circle. Say the words.**

1.

(hospital)   gas station

2.

bank   drugstore

3.

gas station   supermarket

4.

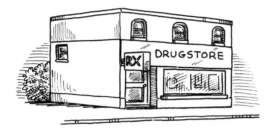

library   post office

5.

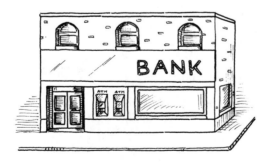

bank   movie theater

G **Match.**

____d____ 1.    **a.** bus stop

_____ 2.    **b.** laundromat

_____ 3.    **c.** movie theater

_____ 4.    ~~**d.**~~ park

_____ 5.    **e.** restaurant

H **Listen. Write g, p, or x.**

1. Where are you __g__oing?

   I'm __oing to the bus sto__.

2. E__cuse me. Where's Isabel?

   She's in the __ost office.

IN, ON, NEXT TO		
In	On	Next to
They are **in** a restaurant.	The bank is **on** the corner.	The drugstore is **next to** the park.

Listen and repeat.

J Match.

___d___ 1. The movie theater is   a. on Lake Avenue.

_____ 2. The park is   b. in the park.

_____ 3. The restaurant is   c. next to the bank.

_____ 4. The man and dog are   d. next to the restaurant.

_____ 5. The drugstore is   e. on 61st Street.

K **Read.**

A Supermarket Card

Card Club Application

A V I L A   C A R L O S
Last Name   First Name

2 1   1 7 T H   A V E N U E
Street Address

L O S   A N G E L E S   C A   9 0 0 2 1
City   State   Zip Code

8 1 8 - 5 5 5 - 0 0 1 2   ▸ *Carlos Avila*   10/14/2010
Home Phone   Applicant's Signature   Date

L **Write about you.**

SUNNY SUPERMARKET   **Card Club** Application

Last Name   First Name

Street Address

City   State   Zip Code

Home Phone   ▸ Applicant's Signature   Date

A **Listen.**

1.

headache

2.

stomachache

3.

backache

4.

toothache

5.

cold

6.

sore throat

Listen and repeat.

B **Circle. Say the word.**

1.

(headache)   backache

2.

toothache   cold

C **Read.**

1. head
2. eye
3. nose
4. stomach
5. arm
6. hand
7. finger
8. leg
9. foot

D **Circle.**

1.

2.

3.

(head)   mouth   eye

hand   nose   finger

arm   leg   hand

E **Match.**

1. arm
2. eye
3. finger
4. head
5. stomach

F. Write.

1.  What's the matter with Ben?

   His ___hand___ hurts.

2.  What's the matter with Leo?

   His _____ hurts.

3.  What's the matter with Ana?

   Her _____ hurts.

G. Read.

Patient: <u>Andy Johnson</u>

Appointment with: ___Dr. Wall___

At: ___6:00___

Dr. Brown will see: <u>Ana Lopez</u>

<u>Wednesday</u> at ___10:00___

H. ✔Check.

	True	False
1. Andy has an appointment with Dr. Brown.		✔
2. Ana has an appointment with Dr. Brown.		
3. Andy's appointment is at 6:00.		
4. Ana's appointment is on Monday.		

 **I Listen.**

1.

cut $\longrightarrow$ bandage

2.

cough $\longrightarrow$ cough syrup

3.

infection $\longrightarrow$ antibiotic

4.

headache $\longrightarrow$ aspirin

Listen and repeat.

J Match.

_C_ 1.   a. headache

___ 2.   b. cough

___ 3.   c. cut

ACTION VERBS	
I	run.
You	run.
We	run.
They	run.
He	run**s**.
She	run**s**.

Listen and repeat.

L Write.

play   1. He _____*plays*_____ soccer.

run   2. We _____.

walk   3. They _____.

swim   4. She _____.

M **Read.**

Be Healthy

exercise

drink water

walk

eat healthy food

N **Write about you.**

1. I ___drink water___ every day.

2. I _____ twice a week.

A Listen.

1.

delivery person

2.

taxi driver

3.

health aide

4.

waiter

5.

cook

6.

cashier

7.

construction
worker

8.

office worker

9.

sales clerk

Listen and repeat.

B Write. Say the word.

1. _c o o k_

2. _____

C **Match.**

___d___ 1. 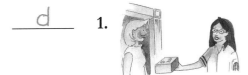   a. construction worker

_____ 2.    b. office worker

_____ 3.    c. waiter

_____ 4.    d̶. delivery person

 D **Listen.**

1.

pots and pans

2.

a taxi

3.

a computer

4.

a cash register

Listen and repeat.

E Match.

___b___ 1. cashier

_____ 2. cook

_____ 3. taxi driver

_____ 4. office worker

a. computer

b. cash register

c. taxicab

d. pots and pans

F Read.

1.

drive

2.

use

3.

sell

4.

fix

G **Listen and circle.**

1. Leo can ⟨drive a car.⟩ use pots and pans.

2. Maria can sell sweaters. drive a car.

3. Ben can fix houses. use a computer.

4. Isabel can use a computer. use a cash register.

H **Read.**

			True	False

I **Read and ✔ check.**

		True	False
1.	This is Nadira Shaheed's paycheck.	✔	
2.	Nadira works for Health Works, Inc.		
3.	The check is for $82.25.		
4.	Nadira makes $9.00 an hour.		
5.	Nadira works 10 hours.		

CAN/CAN'T	
Can you **drive** a car?	Yes, I can.
Can you **use** a cash register?	No, I can't.

Listen and repeat.

K Write.

1. Can Leo drive a car? Ye_s_, he _c_an.

2. Can he fix a computer? N__, he ca__'t.

L ✔Check.

	Can	Can't
Can you drive a car?		
Can you use a computer?		
Can you fix a house?		
Can you sell coats?		

M Read.

```
                                        Human Resources
                                        JOB APPLICATION
 PERSONAL INFORMATION
 Name    Leo Danov

 Address   17 Water Street    City Los Angeles,   State CA      Zip Code 90001

 Telephone 312-555-6533


 I can  _X_ drive a car

        ___ use a computer

        ___ use a cash register

        ___ fix machines

        _X_ speak English and Russian


                    Signature  Leo Danov          Date February 15, 2010
```

N Write about you.

```
                                        Human Resources
                                        JOB APPLICATION
 PERSONAL INFORMATION
 Name

 Address                 City           State        Zip Code

 Telephone


 I can  ___ drive a car

        ___ use a computer

        ___ use a cash register

        ___ fix machines

        ___ speak English _____


                    Signature _____          Date _____
```

A **Listen.**

 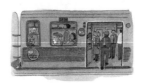 

1. bus   2. bike   3. subway   4. car

Listen and repeat.

B **Match.**

_____b_____ 1. 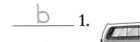   a. bike

_____ 2.   ~~b.~~ bus

_____ 3.   c. car

_____ 4.    d. subway

🎧 **C** **Listen and write.**

1. Leo drives his _____car_____ to school.

2. Will takes a _____ to work.

3. Carlos rides a _____.

4. Paul and Isabel take a _____.

D **Read.**

E **Write _left_ or _right_.**

1. The supermarket is on the _____left_____.

2. The restaurant is on the _____.

3. The hospital is on the _____.

4. The post office is on the _____.

F **Read.**

The supermarket is **on the corner of** Apple Road.
The bank is **across from** the supermarket.
The library is **between** the police station and the drugstore.
The park is **next to** the fire station.

G **Complete the sentences.**

1. The supermarket is _across from_ the bank.

2. The police station is _____ the library.

3. The fire station is between the _____
   and the _____.

4. The bank is _____ B Street.

H Read.

City	Leaves
Chicago	10:15
Miami	11:30
New York	9:00
Sacramento	1:00
Los Angeles	10:45
San Antonio	9:30
Washington, D.C.	1:45

I Match.

___d___ 1. Los Angeles   a. 9:00

_____ 2. San Antonio   b. 9:30

_____ 3. Sacramento   c. 10:15

_____ 4. Washington, D.C.   d. 10:45

_____ 5. New York   e. 11:30

_____ 6. Chicago   f. 1:45

_____ 7. Miami   g. 1:00

J **Listen.**

QUESTIONS WITH *BE*		
Questions		**Short Answers**
What	is the name of your school?	City College.
Where	is the school?	On First Avenue.
When	is your class?	At 8:00 A.M.
Who	is your teacher?	Sandy Johnson.

Listen and repeat.

K **Circle.**

1. When / (Where) is your school?   On Lake Avenue.

2. Where / What is your classmate's name?   Yuri.

3. Who / When is your teacher?   Jon Friedman.

4. What / When is the class?   At 5:00 P.M.

L **Read.**

no parking

hospital

stop

car seat

seat belt

M **Write.**

1. _hospital_

2. _____

3. _____

4. _____

5. _____

Listening Script

Section 1
Letter and Number Practice

Page 2

A. Listen.
T, I, L, H
Listen and repeat.

Page 3

A. Listen.
E, F, A, Y, X
Listen and repeat.

Page 4

A. Listen.
N, M, V, W, K
Listen and repeat.

Page 5

A. Listen and circle.
1. T
2. L
3. A
4. F
5. W
6. N
7. H
8. I
9. Y
10. M

Page 6

A. Listen.
U, C, O, Q
Listen and repeat.

Page 7

A. Listen.
P, R, B, D
Listen and repeat.

Page 8

A. Listen.
S, G, J, Z
Listen and repeat.

Page 9

A. Listen and circle.
1. Q
2. U
3. B
4. R
5. G
6. S
7. O
8. C
9. Z
10. B

Page 10

A. Listen.
l, t, i, j
Listen and repeat.

Page 11

A. Listen.
v, w, x, z
Listen and repeat.

Page 12

A. Listen.
o, c, a, e, s
Listen and repeat.

Page 13

A. Listen and circle.
1. t
2. i
3. w
4. m
5. a
6. o
7. c
8. e

9. x
10. z

Page 14

A. Listen.
u, r, n, h, m
Listen and repeat.

Page 15

A. Listen.
b, d, p, q
Listen and repeat.

Page 16

A. Listen.
y, g, f, k
Listen and repeat.

Page 17

A. Listen and circle.
1. u
2. k
3. d
4. h
5. f
6. j
7. b
8. y
9. p
10. g

Page 18

A. Listen.
A, B, C, D
Listen and repeat.

B. Listen and circle.
1. D
2. A
3. c
4. b

Listening Script

Page 19

A. Listen.
E, F, G, H
Listen and repeat.

B. Listen and circle.
1. G
2. E
3. h
4. f

Page 20

A. Listen.
I, J, K, L
Listen and repeat.

B. Listen and circle.
1. J
2. K
3. i
4. l

Page 21

A. Listen.
M, N, O, P
Listen and repeat.

B. Listen and circle.
1. P
2. M
3. o
4. n

Page 22

A. Listen.
Q, R, S, T, U
Listen and repeat.

B. Listen and circle.
1. R
2. T
3. u
4. s

Page 23

A. Listen.
V, W, X, Y, Z
Listen and repeat.

B. Listen and circle.
1. V
2. Z
3. y
4. w

Page 30

A. Listen.
zero, one, two, three, four, five
Listen and repeat.

Page 31

A. Listen.
six, seven, eight, nine, ten
Listen and repeat.

Page 35

A. Listen.
A, B, C, D, E, F, G, H, I, J, K, L, M
Listen and repeat.

C. Listen.
a, b, c, d, e, f, g, h, i, j, k, l, m
Listen and repeat.

E. Listen and circle.
1. G
2. C
3. h
4. e

Page 36

A. Listen.
N, O, P, Q, R, S, T, U, V, W, X, Y, Z
Listen and repeat.

C. Listen.
n, o, p, q, r, s, t, u, v, w, x, y, z
Listen and repeat.

E. Listen and circle.
1. Z
2. O
3. s
4. u

Page 37

A. Listen.
0, 1, 2, 3, 4, 5, 6, 7, 8, 9, 10
Listen and repeat.

C. Listen and circle.
1. 4
2. 10

Section 2
Phonics Practice
Phonics Practice is on CD 2

Page 40

A. Listen. The letter *b* sounds like /b/. /b/ /b/ book. The letter *d* sounds like /d/. /d/ /d/ desk.
Listen and repeat.

B. Listen for the sounds /b/ and /d/. bus, bat, dish, door.
Listen and repeat.

C. Listen and circle the word you hear.
1. Dan, Dan
2. bug, bug
3. big, big
4. day, day
5. Ben, Ben
6. dark, dark

D. Listen and write *b* or *d*.
1. bag, bag
2. desk, desk
3. book, book
4. day, day
5. door, door
6. box, box
Listen and repeat.

Page 41

A. Listen. The letter *p* sounds like /p/. /p/ /p/ pan. The letter *t* sounds like /t/. /t/ /t/ ten.
Listen and repeat.

141

Listening Script

B. Listen for the sounds /p/ and /t/. pants, pie, tooth, tub.
Listen and repeat.

C. Listen and circle the word you hear.
1. tie, tie
2. ten, ten
3. pin, pin
4. pick, pick
5. pan, pan
6. tail, tail

D. Listen and write *p* or *t*.
1. pink, pink
2. ten, ten
3. talk, talk
4. pot, pot
5. pay, pay
6. tug, tug
Listen and repeat.

Page 42

A. Listen and circle *b*, *d*, *p*, or *t*.
1. boy, boy
2. pen, pen
3. ten, ten
4. desk, desk
5. paper, paper
6. toe, toe
7. dime, dime
8. bell, bell

B. Listen and write *b*, *d*, *p*, or *t*.
1. pie, pie
2. tub, tub
3. dig, dig
4. pat, pat
5. tell, tell
6. dish, dish
7. bed, bed
8. bell, bell
Listen and repeat.

Page 43

A. Listen. The letter *f* sounds like /f/. /f/ /f/ feet. The letter *h* sounds like /h/. /h/ /h/ hand.
Listen and repeat.

B. Listen for the sounds /f/ and /h/. fan, fish, hat, hen.
Listen and repeat.

C. Listen and circle the word you hear.
1. hat, hat
2. fit, fit
3. fall, fall
4. hair, hair
5. here, here
6. fill, fill

D. Listen and write *f* or *h*.
1. he, he
2. five, five
3. fix, fix
4. hello, hello
5. her, her
6. father, father
Listen and repeat.

Page 44

A. Listen. The letter *g* sounds like /g/. /g/ /g/ girl. The letter *j* sounds like /j/. /j/ /j/ jay.
Listen and repeat.

B. Listen for the sounds /g/ and /j/. goat, gas, jug, jacket.
Listen and repeat.

C. Listen and circle the word you hear.
1. go, go
2. gay, gay
3. jot, jot
4. gone, gone
5. job, job
6. jet, jet

D. Listen and write *g* or *j*.
1. gap, gap
2. gas, gas
3. jar, jar
4. jeans, jeans
5. game, game
6. juice, juice
Listen and repeat.

Page 45

A. Listen and circle *f*, *g*, *h*, or *j*.
1. gift, gift
2. jeep, jeep
3. feet, feet
4. hug, hug
5. goose, goose
6. fire, fire
7. jay, jay
8. hen, hen

B. Listen and write *f*, *g*, *h*, or *j*.
1. hat, hat
2. jeep, jeep
3. first, first
4. girl, girl
5. jug, jug
6. get, get
7. hand, hand
8. fish, fish
Listen and repeat.

Page 46

A. Listen. The letter *l* sounds like /l/. /l/ /l/ leg. The letter *r* sounds like /r/. /r/ /r/ rug.
Listen and repeat.

B. Listen for the sounds /l/ and /r/. lamp, lock, rake, rose.
Listen and repeat.

C. Listen and circle the word you hear.
1. lip, lip
2. lay, lay
3. lap, lap
4. rake, rake
5. right, right
6. road, road

D. Listen and write *l* or *r*.
1. read, read
2. land, land
3. run, run
4. look, look
5. list, list
6. red, red
Listen and repeat.

Listening Script

Page 47

A. Listen. The letter *m* sounds like /m/. /m/ /m/ man. The letter *n* sounds like /n/. /n/ /n/ nose.
Listen and repeat.

B. Listen for the sounds /m/ and /n/. map, mug, nine, nest.
Listen and repeat.

C. Listen and circle the word you hear.
1. map, map
2. nine, nine
3. mail, mail
4. net, net
5. noon, noon
6. meet, meet

D. Listen and write *m* or *n*.
1. not, not
2. mat, mat
3. neck, neck
4. may, may
5. near, near
6. make, make
Listen and repeat.

Page 48

A. Listen and circle *l*, *m*, *n*, or *r*.
1. rock, rock
2. list, list
3. money, money
4. nine, nine
5. roof, roof
6. nail, nail
7. lock, lock
8. mail, mail

B. Listen and write *l*, *m*, *n*, or *r*.
1. man, man
2. room, room
3. next, next
4. nose, nose
5. milk, milk
6. rug, rug
7. lunch, lunch
8. large, large
Listen and repeat.

Page 49

A. Listen. The letter *k* sounds like /k/. /k/ /k/ kite. The letters *qu* sound like /kw/. /kw/ /kw/ quilt.
Listen and repeat.

B. Listen for the sounds /k/ and /kw/. key, kilt, queen, quarter.
Listen and repeat.

C. Listen and circle the word you hear.
1. kid, kid
2. quit, quit
3. kale, kale
4. quilt, quilt
5. quick, quick
6. kite, kite

D. Listen and write *k* or *qu*.
1. kiss, kiss
2. quit, quit
3. key, key
4. quick, quick
5. quart, quart
6. keep, keep
Listen and repeat.

Page 50

A. Listen. The letter *v* sounds like /v/. /v/ /v/ van. The letter *w* sounds like /w/. /w/ /w/ watch.
Listen and repeat.

B. Listen for the sounds /v/ and /w/. vest, violin, wiper, window.
Listen and repeat.

C. Listen and circle the word you hear.
1. vet, vet
2. we, we
3. went, went
4. vale, vale
5. vest, vest
6. wow, wow

D. Listen and write *v* or *w*.
1. week, week
2. very, very
3. work, work
4. wet, wet

5. visit, visit
6. vat, vat
Listen and repeat.

Page 51

A. Listen and circle *k*, *qu*, *v*, or *w*.
1. queen, queen
2. vine, vine
3. visor, visor
4. woman, woman
5. key, key
6. water, water
7. quart, quart
8. kite, kite

B. Listen and write *k*, *qu*, *v*, or *w*.
1. van, van
2. walk, walk
3. quiet, quiet
4. kit, kit
5. vest, vest
6. kick, kick
7. quite, quite
8. want, want
Listen and repeat.

Page 52

A. Listen. The letter *x* sounds like /x/. /x/ /x/ fox. The letter *y* sounds like /y/. /y/ /y/ yarn
Listen and repeat.

B. Listen for the sounds /x/ and /y/. six, box, yo-yo, yard.
Listen and repeat.

C. Listen and write *x*.
1. x-ray, x-ray
2. taxi, taxi
3. fix, fix
Listen and repeat.

D. Listen and write *y*.
1. yell, yell
2. yak, yak
3. yardstick, yardstick
Listen and repeat.

Listening Script

Page 53

A. Listen. The letter *s* sounds like/s/. /s/ /s/ sink The letter *z* sounds like/z/. /z/ /z/ zipper.
Listen and repeat.

B. Listen for the sounds /s/ and /z/. sun, six, zip code, zebra.
Listen and repeat.

C. Listen and circle the word you hear.
1. zoo, zoo
2. zip, zip
3. sag, sag
4. sink, sink
5. zing, zing
6. zipper, zipper

D. Listen and write *s* or *z*.
1. sofa, sofa
2. sit, sit
3. zoom, zoom
4. zone, zone
5. sister, sister
6. zero, zero
Listen and repeat.

Page 54

A. Listen. The letter *c* sounds like /k/. /k/ /k/ cap. The letter *c* can also sound like /s/. /s/ /s/ circle.
Listen and repeat.

B. Listen for the sounds /k/ and /s/. cat, corn, city, cent.
Listen and repeat.

C. Listen and write *c*.
1. can, can
2. cook, cook
3. city, city
4. circle, circle
5. cube, cube
6. cell, cell
Listen and repeat.

Page 55

A. Listen and circle *c*, *s*, *x*, *y*, or *z*.
1. box, box
2. yard, yard
3. cell phone, cell phone
4. yak, yak
5. comb, comb
6. zero, zero
7. cent, cent
8. x-ray, x-ray
9. zip code, zip code
10. cube, cube

B. Listen and write *c*, *s*, *x*, *y*, or *z*.
1. mix, mix
2. your, your
3. say, say
4. cold, cold
5. zip, zip
6. next, next
7. cent, cent
8. young, young
Listen and repeat.

Page 56

A. Listen. Short *a* sounds like /a/. /a/ /a/ ant, man, pan, cap.
Listen and repeat.

B. Listen and check the picture when you hear /a/.
1. egg, egg
2. can, can
3. pen, pen
4. hat, hat
5. apple, apple
6. ten, ten

C. Listen and write *a*.
1. am, am
2. last, last
3. class, class
4. address, address
Listen and repeat.

Page 57

A. Listen. Short *e* sounds like /e/. /e/ /e/ egg, pen, desk, leg.
Listen and repeat.

B. Listen and check the picture when you hear /e/.
1. bat, bat
2. seven, seven
3. ten, ten
4. cap, cap
5. jet, jet
6. bell, bell

C. Listen and write *e*.
1. end, end
2. exit, exit
3. men, men
4. cell, cell
Listen and repeat.

Page 58

A. Listen and circle *a* or *e*.
1. mat, mat
2. bed, bed
3. leg, leg
4. van, van

B. Listen and circle the word you hear.
1. end, end
2. pan, pan
3. den, den
4. man, man
5. beg, beg
6. Tex, Tex
7. ham, ham
8. mat, mat

C. Listen and write *a* or *e*.
1. red, red
2. and, and
3. bell, bell
4. ten, ten
5. man, man
6. pack, pack
Listen and repeat.

Listening Script

Page 59

A. Listen. Short *i* sounds like /i/.
/i/ /i/ dish, sit, pill, six.
Listen and repeat.

B. Listen and check the picture
when you hear /i/.
1. pin, pin
2. quilt, quilt
3. desk, desk
4. fix, fix
5. nickel, nickel
6. cat, cat

C. Listen and write *i*.
1. it, it
2. in, in
3. his, his
4. list, list
Listen and repeat.

Page 60

A. Listen. Short *o* sounds like
/o/. /o/ /o/ sock, cot, box, clock.
Listen and repeat.

B. Listen and check the picture
when you hear /o/.
1. log, log
2. can, can
3. pot, pot
4. stop, stop
5. bottle, bottle
6. pen, pen

C. Listen and write *o*.
1. on, on
2. hot, hot
3. job, job
4. stop, stop
Listen and repeat.

Page 61

A. Listen. Short *u* sounds like
/u/. /u/ /u/ bus, tub, nut, rug.
Listen and repeat.

B. Listen and check the picture
when you hear /u/.
1. box, box
2. jug, jug
3. bun, bun
4. cup, cup
5. pill, pill
6. lunch, lunch

C. Listen and write *u*.
1. us, us
2. up, up
3. sun, sun
4. lunch, lunch
Listen and repeat.

Page 62

A. Listen and circle *i, o,* or *u*.
1. cup, cup
2. pill, pill
3. tub, tub
4. pit, pit
5. cot, cot
6. lock, lock

B. Listen and circle the word
you hear.
1. on, on
2. fin, fin
3. cut, cut
4. fix, fix
5. rub, rub
6. nut, nut
7. sock, sock
8. big, big
9. doll, doll

C. Listen and write *i, o,* or *u*.
1. rock, rock
2. pot, pot
3. big, big
4. bus, bus
5. hug, hug
6. up, up
7. fix, fix
8. clock, clock
Listen and repeat.

Page 63

A. Listen and write *a, e, i, o,*
or *u*.
1. pants, pants
2. gift, gift
3. pot, pot
4. desk, desk
5. bell, bell
6. tub, tub
7. bus, bus
8. box, box
9. jacket, jacket
10. lunch, lunch
11. twelve, twelve
12. nickel, nickel

Section 3
Support Exercises for
Student Book
Section 3 is on CD 1

Page 68

A. Listen.
F, L, N
Listen and repeat.

Page 69

D. Listen and circle.
1. LAST
2. name
3. First

Page 70

G. Listen.
1. student
2. teacher
3. book
4. notebook
5. pen
6. backpack
Listen and repeat.

Listening Script

Page 72

K. Listen.
Ben: I'm from China.
Grace: I am from China, too.
Sandy: It's a computer.
Paul: It is a computer.
Nadira: What's this?
Carlos: What is this?
Listen and repeat.

Page 74

A. Listen.
C, S, Z
Listen and repeat.

Page 75

D. Listen and circle.
1. state
2. zip
3. city

Page 76

G. Listen.
1. single
2. married
3. divorced
4. widowed
Listen and repeat.

Page 78

K. Listen.
Am, Is, Are
I am from Somalia.
He is from Somalia.
She is from Somalia.
They are from Somalia.
Listen and repeat.

Page 80

A. Listen.
H, M, Y
Listen and repeat.

Page 81

D. Listen and circle.
1. yes
2. family
3. mother

Page 83

I. Listen.
My name is Mary.
My mother's name is Yoko.
My father's name is Harry.
My brother's name is Mike.
This is my family.
Listen and repeat.

Page 84

L. Listen.
My, Your, His, Her
Sandy: My name is Sandy.
Tien: Your name is Leo.
Maria: His name is Paul.
Grace: Her name is Isabel.
Listen and repeat.

Page 86

A. Listen.
B, D, R
Listen and repeat.

Page 87

E. Listen.
1. bathroom
2. bed
3. tub
4. dining room
5. dresser
6. window
7. rug
8. refrigerator
9. shower
Listen and repeat.

Page 89

H. Listen and circle.
1. bathroom
2. dining room
3. bedroom
4. sink
5. fireplace

Page 90

J. Listen.
Singular and Plural Nouns
Singular
one sofa, one shower
Plural
two sofas, four showers
Listen and repeat.

Page 92

A. Listen.
A, E, T
Listen and repeat.

Page 93

E. Listen and circle.
1. Tuesday
2. Monday
3. Saturday
4. Friday
5. Wednesday
6. Thursday

Page 96

J. Listen.
Simple Present Tense
I walk.
We walk.
You walk.
They walk.
He walks.
She walks.
Listen and repeat.

Listening Script

Page 98

A. Listen.
J, K, Q
Listen and repeat.

Page 99

D. Listen.
1. dress
2. sweater
3. shoes
4. suit
5. shirt
6. pants
7. jacket
8. watch
Listen and repeat.

Page 100

G. Listen.
1. a penny, one cent
2. a nickel, five cents
3. a dime, ten cents
4. a quarter, twenty-five cents
5. a dollar
6. five dollars
Listen and repeat.

Page 102

J. Listen.
Adjectives and Nouns
Adjectives
small, medium, large
Nouns
shirt, shirt, shirt
Adjectives and Nouns
a small shirt
a medium shirt
a large shirt
Listen and repeat.

Page 104

A. Listen.
O, U, V
Listen and repeat.

Page 105

F. Listen.
1. potatoes
2. apples
3. beef
4. chicken
5. butter
6. carrots
Listen and repeat.

Page 107

I. Listen and circle.
1. chicken
2. bread
3. milk
4. apples

Page 108

L. Listen.
Count Nouns
Singular
a carrot, one carrot,
Plural
carrots
Listen and repeat.

Page 110

A. Listen.
I, W
Listen and repeat.

Page 111

D. Listen.
1. It's sunny.
2. It's snowing.
3. It's raining.
4. It's windy.
Listen and repeat.

Page 113

H. Listen and write _i_ or _w_.
1. Nadira likes walking and reading.
2. My name is Isabel. I like swimming.
3. Paul likes playing soccer.
4. Leo likes cooking and watching TV.
5. Tien likes watching TV and walking, too.
6. Carlos likes listening to music.

Page 114

J. Listen.
Present Continuous Tense
I am eating.
He is eating.
She is eating.
We are eating.
You are eating.
They are eating.
Listen and repeat.

Page 116

A. Listen.
G, P, X
Listen and repeat.

Page 117

E. Listen.
supermarket
bank
drugstore
hospital
post office
gas station
library
Listen and repeat.

Page 119

H. Listen and write _g_, _p_ or _x_.
1. Where are you going?
   I'm going to the bus stop.
2. Excuse me. Where's Isabel?
   She's in the post office.

Listening Script

Page 120

I. Listen.
In, On, Next To
In. They are in a restaurant.
On. The bank is on the corner.
Next to. The drugstore is next to the park.
Listen and repeat.

Page 122

A. Listen.
1. headache
2. stomachache
3. backache
4. toothache
5. cold
6. sore throat
Listen and repeat.

Page 125

I. Listen.
1. cut, bandage
2. cough, cough syrup
3. infection, antibiotic
4. headache, aspirin
Listen and repeat.

Page 126

K. Listen.
Action Verbs
I run.
You run.
We run.
They run.
He runs.
She runs.
Listen and repeat.

Page 128

A. Listen.
1. delivery person
2. taxi driver
3. health aide
4. waiter
5. cook
6. cashier
7. construction worker
8. office worker
9. sales clerk
Listen and repeat.

Page 129

D. Listen.
1. pots and pans
2. a taxi
3. a computer
4. a cash register
Listen and repeat.

Page 131

G. Listen and circle.
1. Leo can drive a car.
2. Maria can sell sweaters.
3. Ben can fix houses.
4. Isabel can use a computer.

Page 132

J. Listen.
Can/Can't
Man: Can you drive a car?
Tien: Yes, I can.
Man: Can you use a cash register?
Tien: No, I can't.
Listen and repeat.

Page 134

A. Listen.
1. bus
2. bike
3. subway
4. car
Listen and repeat.

Page 135

C. Listen and write.
1. Leo drives his car to school.
2. Will takes a bus to work.
3. Carlos rides a bike.
4. Paul and Isabel take a train.

Page 138

J. Listen.
Questions with *Be*
Ubah: What is the name of your school?
Nadira: City College.
Ubah: Where is the school?
Nadira: On First Avenue.
Ubah: When is your class?
Nadira: At 8 a.m.
Ubah: Who is your teacher?
Nadira: Sandy Johnson.
Listen and repeat.

Answer Key

Page 5

A. Listen and circle.
1. T
2. L
3. A
4. F
5. W
6. N
7. H
8. I
9. Y
10. M

Page 9

A. Listen and circle.
1. Q
2. U
3. B
4. R
5. G
6. S
7. O
8. C
9. Z
10. B

Page 13

A. Listen and circle.
1. t
2. i
3. w
4. m
5. a
6. o
7. c
8. e
9. x
10. z

Page 17

A. Listen and circle.
1. u
2. k
3. d
4. h
5. f

6. j
7. b
8. y
9. p
10. g

Page 18

B. Listen and circle.
1. D
2. A
3. c
4. b

Page 19

B. Listen and circle.
1. G
2. E
3. h
4. f

Page 20

B. Listen and circle.
1. J
2. K
3. i
4. l

Page 21

B. Listen and circle.
1. P
2. M
3. o
4. n

Page 22

B. Listen and circle.
1. R
2. T
3. u
4. s

Answer Key

Page 23

B. Listen and circle.
1. V
2. Z
3. y
4. w

Page 24

A. Match
1. c
2. d
3. a
4. b

B. Match
1. e
2. d
3. b
4. c
5. a

Page 25

A. Circle the lowercase letter.
1. n
2. f
3. l
4. a

B. Circle the lowercase letter.
1. h
2. r
3. e
4. g

C. Circle the lowercase letter.
1. d
2. t
3. q
4. b
5. r

Page 26

A. Circle the letter.
1. (A)ND   CH(A)IR   T(A)LL
2. (B)LUE   (B)OY   NOTE(B)OOK
3. (C)LASS   NI(C)E   (C)OPY
4. (D)ESK   (D)OOR   BOAR(D)

B. Circle the letter.
1. (E)IGHT   PAP(E)R   P(E)N
2. (F)IVE   (F)IRST   (F)OUR
3. (G)RACE   EIGHT   (G)O
4. (H)I   P(H)ONE   T(H)REE

C. Circle the letter.
1. (I)S   N(I)CE   TH(I)S
2. (J)AR   (J)OB   (J)OHNSON
3. (K)EY   TA(K)E   TAL(K)
4. (L)AST   CLASS   C(L)OSE
5. (M)Y   (M)EET   NA(M)E

Page 27

A. Circle the letter.
1. (N)O   (N)AME   O(N)
2. (O)NE   P(O)INT   Y(O)U
3. (P)EN   (P)ARK   O(P)EN
4. (Q)UICK   (Q)UIT   (Q)UEEN

B. Circle the letter.
1. (R)ED   MA(R)IA   YOU(R)
2. (S)TREET   CARLO(S)   DE(S)K
3. (T)WO   WHA(T)   (T)IEN
4. (U)SA   BL(U)E   P(U)T

C. Circle the letter.
1. (V)ERY   FI(V)E   LI(V)E
2. (W)ALK   (W)HAT   (W)EEK
3. SI(X)   E(X)IT   TA(X)I
4. (Y)ES   (Y)OUR   SA(Y)
5. (Z)ERO   SI(Z)E   (Z)IP CODE

Page 28

A. Circle the letter.
1. (a)nd   Chin(a)   t(a)ll
2. (b)lue   num(b)er   (b)oy
3. (c)opy   (c)hair   ni(c)e
4. (d)o   (d)oor   an(d)

B. Circle the letter.
1. (e)mail   pap(e)r   p(e)n
2. (f)ive   (f)irst   o(f)
3. (g)o   ei(g)ht   walkin(g)
4. (h)ello   p(h)one   w(h)at

C. Circle the letter.
1. (i)s   ni(c)e   h(i)
2. (j)ump   (j)ob   (j)acket
3. tal(k)   boo(k)   (k)itchen
4. (l)ast   c(l)ass   (l)unch

Answer Key

Page 29

A. Circle the letter.
1. (m)y   (m)eet   na(m)e
2. (n)o   (n)ame   o(n)
3. (o)ne   y(o)ur   y(o)u
4. (p)en   co(p)y   o(p)en
5. (q)uick   (q)uit   (q)uarter

B. Circle the letter.
1. (r)ed   (r)oom   you(r)
2. (s)top   (s)peak   de(s)k
3. (t)wo   wha(t)   (t)hree
4. (u)p   yo(u)   p(u)t

C. Circle the letter.
1. se(v)en   fi(v)e   li(v)e
2. (w)rite   bro(w)n   (w)eek
3. ta(x)i   si(x)   Me(x)ico
4. (y)es   (y)our   sa(y)
5. (z)ero   si(z)e   (z)ip code

Page 32

A. Circle.

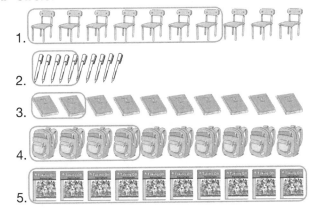

B. Match.
1. c
2. e
3. a
4. b
5. d

Page 33

A. Circle.
1. 2
2. 0
3. 3
4. 7
5. 3
6. 9
7. 8
8. 1
9. 10
10. 4

Page 34

A. Circle.
1. 3
2. 1
3. 7
4. 5
5. 9

Page 35

B. Write.
A B C D E F G H I J K L M

D. Write.
a b c d e f g h i j k l m

E. Listen and circle.
1. G
2. C
3. h
4. e

Page 36

B. Write.
N O P Q R S T U V W X Y Z

D. Write.
n o p q r s t u v w x y z

E. Listen and circle.
1. Z
2. O
3. s
4. u

Page 37

B. Write.
0 1 2 3 4 5 6 7 8 9 10

Answer Key

C. Listen and circle.
1. 4
2. 10

Page 40

C. Listen and circle.
1. Dan
2. bug
3. big
4. day
5. Ben
6. dark

D. Listen and write *b* or *d*.
1. bag
2. desk
3. book
4. day
5. door
6. box

Page 41

C. Listen and circle.
1. tie
2. ten
3. pin
4. pick
5. pan
6. tail

D. Listen and write *p* or *t*.
1. pink
2. pen
3. talk
4. pot
5. pay
6. tug

Page 42

A. Listen and circle *b*, *d*, *p*, or *t*.
1. b
2. p
3. t
4. d
5. p
6. t
7. d
8. b

B. Listen and write *b*, *d*, *p*, or *t*.
1. pie
2. tub
3. dig
4. pat
5. tell
6. dish
7. bed
8. bell

Page 43

C. Listen and circle.
1. hat
2. fit
3. fall
4. hair
5. here
6. fill

D. Listen and write *f* or *h*.
1. he
2. five
3. fix
4. hello
5. her
6. father

Page 44

C. Listen and circle.
1. go
2. gay
3. jot
4. gone
5. job
6. jet

D. Listen and write *g* or *j*.
1. gap
2. gas
3. jar
4. jeans
5. game
6. juice

Page 45

A. Listen and circle *f*, *g*, *h*, or *j*.
1. g
2. j

Answer Key

3. f
4. h
5. g
6. f
7. j
8. h

B. Listen and write *f*, *g*, *h*, or *j*.

1. hat
2. jeep
3. first
4. girl
5. jug
6. get
7. hand
8. fish

Page 46

C. Listen and circle.

1. lip
2. lay
3. lap
4. rake
5. right
6. road

D. Listen and write *l* or *r*.

1. read
2. land
3. run
4. look
5. list
6. red

Page 47

C. Listen and circle.

1. map
2. nine
3. mail
4. net
5. noon
6. meet

D. Listen and write *m* or *n*.

1. not
2. mat
3. neck
4. may
5. near
6. make

Page 48

A. Listen and circle *l*, *m*, *n*, or *r*.

1. r
2. l
3. m
4. n
5. r
6. n
7. l
8. m

B. Listen and write *l*, *m*, *n*, or *r*.

1. man
2. room
3. next
4. nose
5. milk
6. rug
7. lunch
8. large

Page 49

C. Listen and circle.

1. kid
2. quit
3. kale
4. quilt
5. quick
6. kite

D. Listen and write *k* or *qu*.

1. kiss
2. quit
3. key
4. quick
5. quart
6. keep

Page 50

C. Listen and circle.

1. vet
2. we
3. went
4. vale
5. vest
6. wow

153

Answer Key

D. Listen and write _v_ or _w_.
1. week
2. very
3. work
4. wet
5. visit
6. vat

Page 51

A. Listen and circle _k_, _qu_, _v_, or _w_.
1. qu
2. v
3. v
4. w
5. k
6. w
7. qu
8. k

B. Listen and write _k_, _qu_, _v_, or _w_.
1. van
2. walk
3. quiet
4. kit
5. vest
6. kick
7. quite
8. want

Page 52

C. Listen and write _x_.
1. x-ray
2. taxi
3. fix

D. Listen and write _y_.
1. yell
2. yak
3. yardstick

Page 53

C. Listen and circle.
1. zoo
2. zip
3. sag
4. sink
5. zing
6. zipper

D. Listen and write _s_ or _z_.
1. sofa
2. sit
3. zoom
4. zone
5. sister
6. zero

Page 54

C. Listen and write _c_.
1. can
2. cook
3. city
4. circle
5. cube
6. cell

Page 55

A. Listen and circle _c_, _s_, _x_, _y_, or _w_.
1. x
2. y
3. c
4. y
5. c
6. z
7. c
8. x
9. z
10. c

B. Listen and write _c_, _s_, _x_, _y_, or _w_.
1. mix
2. your
3. say
4. cold
5. zip
6. next
7. cent _or_ sent
8. young

Page 56

B. Listen and check.
1. no check
2. ✔
3. no check
4. ✔

Answer Key

5. ✔
6. no check

C. Listen and write *a*.
1. am
2. last
3. class
4. address

Page 57

B. Listen and check.
1. no check
2. ✔
3. ✔
4. no check
5. ✔
6. ✔

C. Listen and write *e*.
1. end
2. exit
3. men
4. cell

Page 58

A. Listen and circle *a* or *e*.
1. a
2. e
3. e
4. a

B. Listen and circle.
1. end
2. pan
3. den
4. man
5. beg
6. Tex
7. ham
8. mat

C. Listen and write *a* or *e*.
1. red
2. and
3. bell
4. ten
5. man
6. pack

Page 59

B. Listen and check.
1. ✔
2. ✔
3. no check
4. ✔
5. ✔
6. no check

C. Listen and write *i*.
1. it
2. in
3. his
4. list

Page 60

B. Listen and check.
1. ✔
2. no check
3. ✔
4. ✔
5. ✔
6. no check

C. Listen and write *o*.
1. on
2. hot
3. job
4. stop

Page 61

B. Listen and check.
1. no check
2. ✔
3. ✔
4. ✔
5. no check
6. ✔

C. Listen and write *u*.
1. us
2. up
3. sun
4. lunch

Answer Key

Page 62

A. Listen and circle *i*, *o*, or *u*.
1. u
2. i
3. u
4. i
5. o
6. o

B. Listen and circle.
1. on
2. fin
3. cut
4. fix
5. rub
6. nut
7. sock
8. big
9. doll

C. Listen and write *i*, *o*, or *u*.
1. rock
2. pot
3. big
4. bus
5. hug
6. up
7. fix
8. clock

Page 63

A. Listen and write *a*, *e*, *i*, *o*, or *u*.
1. pants
2. gift
3. pot
4. desk
5. bell
6. tub
7. bus
8. box
9. jacket
10. lunch
11. twelve
12. nickel

Page 68

B. Write.
1. FIRST; four
2. CLOSE; listen
3. NAME; nice

C. Circle.
1. (FIRST)   FIVE   FOUR
2. LIST   LEFT   (LAST)
3. nine   (name)   meet
4. book   computer   (notebook)

Page 69

D. Listen and circle.
1. LAST
2. name
3. First

E. Circle *NAME* and *name*.

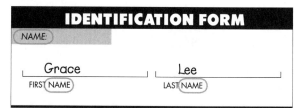

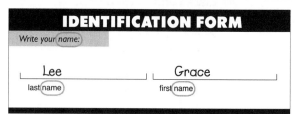

F. Write. Say the word.
1. FIRST   first   FIRST
2. LAST   last   LAST
3. name   NAME   name

Page 70

H. Circle. Say the word.
1. book   (backpack)   student
2. student   pen   (book)
3. (notebook)   student   teacher
4. backpack   notebook   (pen)

Answer Key

Page 71

I. Write.
1. book
2. student
3. backpack
4. teacher

J. Write.
1. Lam; Tien
2. Danov; Leo

Page 72

L. Match.
1. b
2. c
3. a

M. Write.
1. I am from China
2. I'm from Mexico.
3. What is this?
4. It's a backpack.
5. What's this?
6. It is a notebook.

Page 74

B. Write.
1. CITY   country
2. STREET   six
3. ZERO   zoo

C. Circle. Say the word.
1. CODE   CLOSE   (COLOR)
2. STAY   (STREET)   STOP
3. (zip)   sip   zap
4. zone   nose   (zero)

Page 75

D. Listen and circle.
1. state
2. zip
3. city

E. Circle CITY and City.

1.
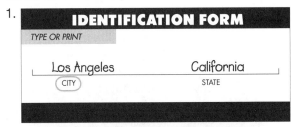

2.

F. Circle STATE and State.

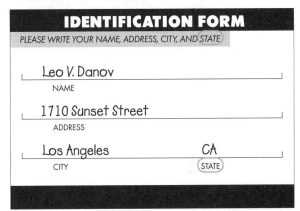

Page 76

H. Check.
1. Single
2. Widowed
3. Divorced
4. Married

157

Answer Key

Page 77

I. Match.

address: Maria Cruz
20 Paper Street
Los Angeles, California 90011
city: Los Angeles
name: Maria Cruz
state: California
zip code: 90011

J. Write.

IDENTIFICATION FORM

TYPE OR PRINT

Lemat	Paul	S.
LAST NAME	FIRST NAME	MI

10 Pen Street	Los Angeles	CA	90015
ADDRESS	CITY	STATE	ZIP CODE

Page 78

L. Match.
1. b
2. c
3. a

Page 79

N. Write the states.
A – M: California
Illinois
Colorado
Florida
Minnesota
N – Z: New York
Oregon
Texas

Page 80

B. Write.
1. HER   his
2. MOTHER   family
3. YOUNG   pretty

C. Circle. Say the word.
1. (HIS)   HIT   HIM
2. MISTER   (MOTHER)   MATTER

3. year   (your)   yes
4. (husband)   how   help

Page 81

D. Listen and circle.
1. yes
2. family
3. mother

E. Match.
1. d
2. c
3. b
4. a

Page 82

G. Check.
1. family
2. children

H. Circle.
1. daughter
2. father
3. mother
4. son

Page 83

J. Write. Say the sentence.
1. My name is Mary.
2. My mother's name is Yoko.
3. My father's name is Harry.
4. My brother's name is Mike.
5. This is my family.

Page 84

M. Circle.
1. Ms.   (My)   Mr.
2. YARN   YOU   (YOUR)
3. (his)   hit   ham
4. Has   Hair   (Her)

N. Write.
1. My name is Sandy.
2. Your name is Leo.
3. His name is Paul.
4. Her name is Isabel.

Answer Key

Page 85

P. Write.
1. married
2. mother
3. grandmother
4. relatives

Page 86

B. Write.
1. BEDROOM   bed
2. DRESSER   desk
3. ROOM   rug

C. Circle. Say the word.
1. (BED)   BAD   DAB
2. ROOM   (DOOR)   DO
3. red   dear   (read)
4. dress   (dresser)   dresses

Page 87

D. Match.
1. c
2. d
3. e
4. a
5. b

Page 88

F. Check.
1. bed
2. shower
3. bathroom
4. window
5. tub
6. refrigerator

G. Write b, d, or r. Say the word.
1. rug
2. door
3. dresser
4. bathroom
5. refrigerator

Page 89

H. Listen and circle.
1. bathroom
2. dining room
3. bedroom
4. sink
5. fireplace

I. Check.

	Kitchen	Living Room	Bedroom	Bathroom
1. bed			✔	
2. dresser			✔	
3. refrigerator	✔			
4. rug		✔		
5. sofa		✔		
6. tub				✔

Page 90

K. Check.
1. 4 windows
2. 1 tub
3. 2 beds
4. 1 rug

Page 91

M. Write.
1. Tien is at home.
2. Her apartment building has 6 floors.
3. Her apartment is number 305.
4. It has a balcony.

Page 92

B. Write.
1. APRIL   Monday
2. ENGLISH   read
3. TUESDAY   time

C. Circle.
1. APPLE   (APRIL)   PAPER
2. (EVERY)   EVER   NEVER
3. (Thursday)   Thirsty   Tuesday
4. tame   (time)   mite

Answer Key

Page 93

D. Match.
1. d
2. b
3. f
4. g
5. e
6. a
7. c

E. Listen and circle.
1. Tuesday
2. Monday
3. Saturday
4. Friday
5. Wednesday
6. Thursday

Page 94

F. Match.
1. f
2. c
3. e
4. a
5. d
6. b

G. Match.
1. b
2. c
3. e
4. a
5. d
6. f

Page 95

H. Check.

	Day	Month
1. August		✔
2. Wednesday	✔	
3. Thursday	✔	
4. October		✔
5. July		✔
6. Saturday	✔	

I. Circle the month.

Page 96

K. Write.
1. He listens to music every day.
2. I swim every day.
3. She reads every day.
4. We talk on the phone every day.

Page 97

M. Write.
1. It is a birthday party for Isabel.
2. Isabel is 21.
3. The party is on Saturday.
4. The party is in May.

Page 98

B. Write.
1. JUNE   jacket
2. CLERK   sneakers
3. QUICK   quarter

C. Circle. Say the word.
1. JANUARY   TICKET   (JACKET)
2. SICK   (SOCK)   SACK
3. quit   queen   (quilt)
4. jacket   (job)   jog

Page 99

E. Match.
1. c
2. a

Answer Key

3. b
4. d

Page 100

F. **Circle. Say the word.**
   1. sweater
   2. shoes
   3. suit
   4. watch

Page 101

H. **Circle.**
   1. 40¢
   2. $1.25
   3. $2.10

I. **Match.**
   1. b
   2. a
   3. c

Page 102

K. **Check.**

			small	medium	large
1.				✔	
2.			✔		
3.					✔

Page 103

M. **Write.**
   1. Pants are $18.75.
   2. Suits are $62.50.
   3. Two sweaters are $44.

Page 104

B. **Write.**
   1. ONION   orange
   2. SOUP   hungry
   3. VEGETABLE   have

C. **Circle. Say the word.**
   1. OPEN   OVER   ORDER
   2. BETTER   BUTTER   BATTER
   3. have   heavy   hive
   4. old   oil   olive

Page 105

D. **Write the letter. Say the word.**
   1. ORANGE   potatoes
   2. juice   FRUIT
   3. HAVE   vegetable

E. **Match.**
   1. c
   2. a
   3. b

Page 106

G. **Write the number.**

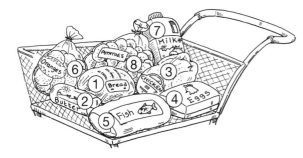

H. **Match.**
   1. d
   2. b
   3. a
   4. e
   5. c

Page 107

I. **Listen and circle.**
   1. chicken
   2. bread

Answer Key

3. milk

4. apples

K. Look at activity J. Circle the aisle.

1. Aisle 1

2. Aisle 3

3. Aisle 2

4. Aisle 2

Page 108

M. Write.

1. apples

2. chickens

3. oranges

4. cakes

Page 109

O. Write a shopping list.

1. juice

2. cereal

3. peanut butter

4. beans

Page 110

B. Write.

1. IT'S	like	spring
2. WEATHER	windy	walk

C. Circle. Say the word.

1. IT'S	IN	(I'M)
2. WAIT	(WALK)	WORK
3. (in)	is	it
4. winter	window	(windy)

Page 111

E. Match.

1. b

2. c

3. d

4. a

Page 112

G. Match.

1. c

2. a

3. d

4. b

Page 113

H. Listen and write *i* or *w*.

1. Nadira likes walking and reading.

2. My name is Isabel. I like swimming.

3. Paul likes playing soccer.

4. Leo likes cooking and watching TV.

5. Tien likes watching TV and walking, too.

6. Carlos likes listening to music.

I. Look at Activity H. Complete.

1. Nadira likes walking and reading.

2. Isabel likes swimming.

3. Paul likes playing soccer.

4. Leo likes cooking and watching TV.

5. Tien likes watching TV and walking, too.

6. Carlos likes listening to music.

Page 114

K. Write *am*, *is*, or *are*.

1. She is reading.

2. They are walking.

3. I am cooking.

4. He is talking.

Page 115

M. Write.

1. It is snowing outside.

2. They are eating lunch.

3. Leo is reading the newspaper.

4. Tien is working on the computer.

5. Nadira is talking on her cell phone.

Page 116

B. Write.

1. GO	group
2. POST OFFICE	police
3. EXCUSE ME	next

C. Circle.

1. GONG	(GOING)	GONE
2. PAL	(PLAY)	PAY
3. tax	(taxi)	taxing
4. part	(park)	pick

Answer Key

Page 117

D. Write the letter. Say the word.
1. GAS STATION   drugstore
2. hospital   SUPERMARKET
3. EXCUSE ME   exit

Page 118

F. Circle. Say the words.
1. hospital
2. drugstore
3. gas station
4. post office
5. bank

Page 119

G. Match.
1. d
2. a
3. b
4. e
5. c

H. Listen and write g, p, or x.
1. Where are you going?
   I'm going to the bus stop.
2. Excuse me. Where's Isabel?
   She's in the post office.

Page 120

J. Match.
1. d
2. e
3. a
4. b
5. c

Page 122

B. Circle. Say the word.
1. headache
2. cold

Page 123

D. Circle.
1. head
2. nose
3. arm

E. Match.
1. arm
2. eye
3. finger
4. head
5. stomach

Page 124

F. Write.
1. His hand hurts.
2. His finger hurts.
3. Her ear hurts.

H. Check.

	True	False
1. Andy has an appointment with Dr. Brown.		✔
2. Ana has an appointment with Dr. Brown.	✔	
3. Andy's appointment is at 6:00.	✔	
4. Ana's appointment is on Monday.		✔

Page 125

J. Match.
1. c
2. b
3. a

Page 126

L. Write.
1. He plays soccer.
2. We run.
3. They walk.
4. She swims.

Page 128

B. Write. Say the word.
1. cook
2. cashier

Answer Key

Page 129

C. **Match.**
1. d
2. c
3. b
4. a

Page 130

E. **Match.**
1. b
2. d
3. c
4. a

Page 131

G. **Listen and circle.**
1. Leo can drive a car.
2. Maria can sell sweaters.
3. Ben can fix houses.
4. Isabel can use a computer.

I. **Read and check.**

		True	False
1.	This is Nadira Shaheed's paycheck.	✔	
2.	Nadira works for Health Works, Inc.	✔	
3.	The check is for $82.25.	✔	
4.	Nadira makes $9.00 an hour.		✔
5.	Nadira works 10 hours.	✔	

Page 132

K. **Write.**
1. Yes, he can.
2. No, he can't

Page 134

B. **Match.**
1. b
2. c
3. d
4. a

Page 135

C. **Listen and write.**
1. Leo drives his car to school.
2. Will takes a bus to work.
3. Carlos rides a bike.
4. Paul and Isabel take a train.

E. **Write _left_ or _right_.**
1. The supermarket is on the left.
2. The restaurant is on the right.
3. The hospital is on the right.
4. The post office is on the left.

Page 136

G. **Complete the sentences.**
1. The supermarket is across from the bank.
2. The police station is next to the library.
3. The fire station is between the bank and the park.
4. The bank is on the corner of B Street.

Page 137

I. **Match.**
1. d
2. b
3. g
4. f
5. a
6. c
7. e

Page 138

K. **Circle.**
1. Where
2. What
3. Who
4. When

Page 139

M. **Write.**
1. hospital
2. seat belt
3. no parking
4. stop
5. car seat